THE GUN SMOKE STILL LINGERS

Ann O'Neill

Author's note on the title
'The Gun Smoke Still Lingers'

During the celebrations held in Amman for my 80th birthday, my niece Christina read out a message she had brought from my brother, Colin.

He wrote, 'In Jullunder we heard the gun salute for the death of the King Emperor George V and watched the gun smoke drift through the trees.' He ended his message with, 'It's a while since the gun smoke'.

His words brought that day in January 1936 so vividly to life and evoked such memories of my youth in India. It is a country I have loved since childhood.
Throughout all my years and all my travels, it has never dimmed.

The call of doves, scent of water on dust, or roadside dung fires and the brilliance of flowers brings India to my mind's eye.

It was many, many years before I travelled there again. As I came out of the airport into that hot, colourful, crowded, noisy scene I felt I had come home.

THE GUN SMOKE STILL LINGERS

ANN O'NEILL

GILGAMESH
PUBLISHING LTD

The Gun Smoke Still Lingers

Copyright text and photographs © Ann O'Neill 2015
All rights reserved.

Published by Gilgamesh Publishing in 2015
Email: info@gilgamesh-publishing.co.uk
www.gilgamesh-publishing.co.uk

ISBN

© Ann O'Neill 2015

CIP Data: A catalogue for this book is
available from the British Library

Tributes

Christina Dunlop, niece to the author:

'The Great Mink', as she is so fondly known to our family, is probably one of the last of a generation of inspirational women made from the same strong tweed cloth. This book brings to life her story, from the heat and intrigue of bygone days of the Indian Raj through to the mystique of the Middle East, intermingled with visits to England. Through her lens and her written word she has passed on to others the wonders of Jordan and given insight into many hidden gems of delight.

Johnny Mackenzie, nephew to the author:

Reading through your journals, Mink, I am reliving these places and stories, so many of which are already familiar to me. You are a demonstrably clear and vivid writer. Your prose reads strongly, your eye for detail is striking and you are good at keeping everything moving along. Overall, there is a wonderful fluidity about these memoirs. They really were such a delight to read!

Remembering with love dearest Colin,
soldier, traveller, countryman, poet ...
who shared so much of life in India.

Ann and Colin in Gulmarg, Kashmir, summer 1943

LIST OF COLOUR ILLUSTRATIONS

ACKNOWLEDGEMENTS

When I first thought of writing a story about my life – so many years ago – I asked my family what they thought of the idea. With one accord they all said, 'Yes'. So began the mammoth task of re-membering and then assembling all the incidents and experiences I had accumulated, together with my impressions and thoughts going back eighty years. It has been a long time in the making, and family and friends have been inexhaustibly patient. For this I thank them all.

From the very first, Colin shared my enthusiasm and was ever encouraging. He would gently press me to continue working, and was always ready to check dates and place names. My warmest thanks to Anne, ready to listen to my stories, and offering practical suggestions about printing. Thank you Christina, for your warm and enthusiastic appraisal of the memoirs, and thank you Johnny, for your interest and for taking the time to read the script and make useful comments.

I owe a great debt of gratitude to Jamal and Elizabeth Qabouq who have had me to stay countless weekends at their lovely farmhouse in the hills outside Jarash. Elizabeth has given unsparingly of her time as we worked for many hours on editing and proofreading. Jamal so kindly scanned my photographs and advised on sizing.

For all the interesting facts about the construction of the 4.8 kilometre Bangabandhu Bridge across the Jamuna River in northern Bangladesh, I thank Michael Taylor most warmly.

There will be others I do not have space to include here, but who are none the less appreciated. You will know who you are and I thank you.

Take a seat and travel with me!

Ann O'Neill, August 2015

FOREWORD

Ann O'Neill's memoir, *The Gun Smoke Still Lingers*, is a thoughtful insight into her work and travels – a remarkable and inspiring account.

I first knew Mrs O'Neill, or Miss Mackenzie as she was then, and Ize, as I nicknamed her soon after she arrived, in 1962, when I was ten years old.

She came to Jordan initially as my governess and shortly afterwards took over as my private tutor. It was mainly because of the way she was able to spark my interest in a variety of subjects that our lessons were far from dull. Ize helped me to discover the joys of reading, introducing me to classics such as *Our Island Story* and *Scotland's Story* by H.E. Marshall. When later I started at Benenden, aged twelve and a half, the care and nurture that Ize provided as my guardian was a tremendous source of support to me and helped me settle into a new environment and way of life.

Young Jordanians have also benefited from her superb teaching. Like me, they have been inspired by her commitment to live to the fullest potential and to strive to create positive change.

When Ann eventually returned to Jordan she embraced it as her home, developing a deep knowledge of the country in every aspect, whether culturally, historically or geographically. Until this day, I cherish childhood memories of trips to the countryside with Ize to look for wild cyclamen and poppies. Her passion for wild flowers spurred her on adventurous expeditions off the beaten track to find and record Jordan's flora. The spirited appreciation of her surroundings characterizes the stories of her world wide journeys, and it is this that makes *The Gun Smoke Still Lingers* such an entertaining read.

The experiences, as well as the discoveries that Ize has made in Jordan, are also reflected in the remarkable collection of photographs from which she produces a unique brand of items that reflect her own take on the beauty and natural diversity of Jordan. She has strong feelings about the need to protect our natural environment from modern-day incursions.

Together with a small group, Ann also commits time to working among both Iraqi and Syrian refugees. The team places a strong emphasis on visiting and getting to know the families.

It gives me tremendous pleasure and pride to recommend this fascinating glimpse into the journeys of Ann O'Neill, my life-long friend. Through all the phases of her work among both Jordanians and non-Jordanians she has earned appreciation and respect. Moreover, she has become a part of the fabric of Jordan on which she continues to make her mark.

HRH Princess Basma bint Talal

1

I was in the middle with an older sister and a younger brother. Both Elizabeth and Colin were born in India and it was always a sore point for me to have been delivered in England. I grew more sanguine in time, knowing that at least I had been conceived in that far-off land and, according to my mother, was almost born on a horse! At birth a bright red horseshoe was imprinted on my forehead – shades of things to come.

Ann, aged 18 months, on Bobby with mother and the orderly, 1931

India, that great subcontinent, was all one country when I was born on 13th March 1930. My father, Fleming Mackenzie, was an Indian Army officer serving with the 15th Punjab Regiment. These regiments were formed of men from mixed races, religions and regions. There were Punjabi Mussalmans, Sikhs – also native to the Punjab – Khattacks from the North West Frontier Province, Pathans from the Afghan border, and Jats – the Hindu soldier class. Each culture with its ethnic differences, manner of worship and varied diets was catered for separately, yet all together they formed a magnificent fighting force and one immensely loyal to the British Crown.

Recruiting was an important part of army life, and on a number of occasions my mother, brother and I accompanied my father to interesting areas of recruitment. The beautiful Kulu Valley, lush with fields of brilliant yellow mustard, was such fun to ride through mounted on rough hill ponies, the foliage tickling our bare legs. At prearranged venues, my father would be seated at a table under the shade of a tree. His chief clerk, as I well recall, was an immaculately turned out Sikh Jemadar, standing beside him and checking the name of each recruit. This was always a personal as well as a serious business for the young men who sought to join the regiment. They had walked several days to be there at the appointed time, and were anxious to follow in the tradition of military service as their fathers and brothers before them. Many had never worn conventional footwear and frequently arrived unshod, although they could handle a rifle with the best.

Once accepted, after medical check-ups, the recruit would go to the training battalion for a six-week initiation period. This involved learning how to put on his uniform and, most importantly, wear his boots. There was instruction in marching and understanding all the orders this involved, as well as the many English words so favoured by sergeant majors. Rifle practice was of course essential, and in this art many of the tribesmen from the wild mountainous country of their birth excelled. Sleeping under canvas, eating at set times and tough competitive sports were all part of the aim to shape a well-balanced, fit and integrated soldier.

The training battalion was in the Punjab at the cantonment in Ambala. The 'lines' where the soldiers lived were all laid out in orderly fashion: rows of tents, cookhouses a little apart for each religious denomination.

At the end of this training period, there was an attestation parade – the culmination of those hard weeks. Before being drafted to their platoons, however, each new soldier swore allegiance to the Crown. The ceremony would take place in the cool of early morning on the parade ground. Every man stood with his own kind, their holy men before them. When called upon to affirm their loyalty, Sikh, Muslim and Jat, each in turn, did so within their own faith. It has always remained so vividly in my mind as I remember the pride with which these such different men all shared one aim. With the band playing the companies marched in perfect formation, and as they passed the King's Colours, 'Eyes right!'

With trouble on the frontier and the blowing up of the Bannu Bridge across the Indus, my father's battalion was sent up there and based in Thal Fort. In the meanwhile, my mother, Colin and I were living in Abbottabad. My mother became really ill with dysentery during our stay, and I well remember, at age six, not only looking after Colin, then aged four, but also trying to keep my mother's forehead cool with constant application of damp flannels. My father's growing concern for her health brought him down to Abbottabad and he took us back with him.

Thal was a frontier fort, but double-walled with smart living quarters and flowerbeds. Like all these forts, it lay very close to the border of Afghanistan and my father sometimes took us outside to visit a picket. These were small stone-built advance posts, shaped like bee hives, no windows, just slits wide enough for a rifle butt. The scene beyond was desolate, mile upon mile of barren, rocky landscape, rolling hills and

Thal Fort, North West Frontier, 1936

deep ravines. This was always the perfect fighting ground for the tribesmen, Pathans, Afridis, Waziris and so many others. History records tales of great bravery and heroism on both sides.

Thal Fort also had a postern gate, used mostly after dusk when the rest of the fort was secured. It was here that Colin discovered the fun of going back and forth through it with the duty sentry duly saluting each time. In due course our father appeared and put a speedy stop to that. We were both fascinated by the chain attached to the sentry's rifle and around his waist, a very necessary precaution with the swift, light-fingered tribesmen adept at creeping out of the dark to snatch another weapon. We spent the Christmas of 1936 here, and I always swear that I saw Father Christmas and his reindeer outside in the snow.

In the new year, we moved once more, this time to Fort Lockhart, another of the defence forts along the North West Frontier. I well remember watching the assembly of mules and camels being loaded with military hardware. Camels carried the gun parts. As a vital means of transport, mules in particular were treated royally. Each animal was in the charge of a sepoy and tethered to a large ring in the ground. Their coats shone with daily brushing and their hooves glistened with oil. But dare you get anywhere near them, they would lash out with their powerful hindquarters or bite you severely. They were immensely strong and transported the ammunition boxes over high passes, rough tracks and along the edges of precipices to Fort Lockhart.

On one occasion whilst we were living in Lockhart, Colin and I tied a balloon to the tail of our Airedale, Peter, and let him loose amongst the mules! Of course he created havoc, with much kicking of heels and swearing of men before the balloon finally burst. Here we lived in tents. On guest nights, the regimental band played for the officers and their ladies while they dined. The bandmaster, Santa Singh, was a striking figure whom we considered our friend. As luck would have it, the band played just outside our tent. Of course we didn't stay in bed. Peter was again pressed into service, and sent out to run amongst the bandsmen – not a dignified scene. We then had the perfect opportunity to rush out and have some more fun trying to catch him before authority caught up with us.

HONY. JEMADAR SANTA SINGH, BANDMASTER
ENLISTED. 1893.
STILL SERVING WITH THE BATTALION

The road to Fort Lockhart, 1936

Bridge over the Kurram River below Thal Fort, 1936

Another winter venue, but a very different one, was Parachinar. At that time it was but a small collection of houses and the headquarters of the District Officer (DO), Andrew Smith. A district in India could be very large (the size of several English counties), and the DO would be required to travel a great deal. Mr Smith's two children were about our ages, and we had great fun building huge snowmen and playing with the Smiths' pet lamb. A cracked and faded snapshot shows all four of us with the lamb, standing in the road, snow walls towering above our heads. How tragic that some sixty years on, Parachinar, once a pinprick on the border with Afghanistan, would become 'home' to tens of thousands of Afghan refugees.

More recruiting took my father up the Kangra Valley to Palampur. The hill station of Palampur was a pretty place lying in the lee of the mountains. That spring the hillsides were smothered in wild hydrangeas, something I'd never seen before or since. I also remember it for something less pleasant: bed bugs! We stayed in a dak bungalow (government rest house) and over successive nights I began scratching frantically. The next morning, nothing could be found. One night my mother came in, switched on the light and caught them at it. They were nocturnal feeders, retreating into the mattress ticking during the day. They could certainly produce mighty large bumps!

Manali, a village high in the mountains, was where my father tried his luck at stalking bear. While he was thus engaged, my mother, brother and I were snow-bound in a very cold bungalow with no electricity. From somewhere my mother produced candles and, over an ancient oil stove, cooked us macaroni. We lived on that for several days until the weather broke, father returned (without a bear) and things became more normal. It's surprising that I can still face those 'drainpipes'.

* * * * *

In October 1938 my father was given command of the escort to the British Trade Agent in Gyantse, Tibet. An unusual and much sought after assignment, this entailed training a small body of men specially chosen from the battalion. They would be living and working at heights of up to 15,000 feet and needed to be extremely tough and fit. Transport at those heights was on small, agile Tibetan ponies, sure-footed in that rugged terrain and inured to the extremes of temperature. Winter was bitter with little movement, the mountains

Typical village in the Kurram Valley, 1936

and valleys blanketed in deep snow, but, as my father described in words and with sketches, spring was a glory of colour. Yaks grazed on the lush hillsides and streams tumbled in cascades, their banks lined with women busy washing piles of winter clothing. A married Tibetan woman was distinguished by her 'married woman's' apron. This, worn over the long black, wide-sleeved dress, was most colourful, in horizontal stripes of every hue. Sporting facilities were very limited, so some of the troops were assigned to level the flattest piece of land to create one of the highest polo grounds in the world at 13,000 feet.

Like many mountain peoples, Tibetans were self-sufficient and produced most of their own daily essentials. The yak provided milk and butter; it was also a pack animal, as well as giving wool for clothing and hide for tents. Above all, Tibetan people had their deeply rooted, sustaining faith. Its expression was part of daily living and every family had at least one son serving in a Buddhist monastery. My father had the good fortune during that year to travel widely and meet with lamas and abbots. Strict ritual was observed for such a visit to the monastery head. A long, white silk scarf lay across the visitor's arms, concealing his hands. On meeting the abbot, the guest would bow his head and intone the time-honoured mantra, 'Om mane padme hum' – 'O, the jewel in the lotus'.

Picnics were a favourite form of entertainment and many families would join forces to cook a meal, then load it onto yaks to be carried high above the village to the flowery pastures. Although alcohol was virtually unknown, a bottle or two of Crème de Menthe went down very well, not only for its taste, but for its brilliant green colour. A rather more acquired taste for the foreign visitor was tea laced with small round balls of yak butter. My father's description and mock grimaces always made us laugh.

He often told me in later years that in all his travels he had never met a truly happier people. Because of his vivid descriptions and lovely black and white drawings of the great Himalayan peaks of Chomolhari and Kanchenjunga, we grew up with a considerable understanding of and deep affection for the land and people of Tibet.

* * * * *

Colin and my father at Old Cleeve House, 1939

At the outbreak of the Second World War in 1939 my father was still serving in India, having moved to Calcutta. The family was living in a Somerset village in a lovely house with a large garden and ponies to ride.

War hardly touched us young ones in the rural West Country of England and the only thing at that time that brought it vaguely home was the arrival of gas masks. Someone from the Home Guard brought them round and I recall us all standing in the garden as the man explained how to put them on. They were in brown cardboard boxes with a cord to hang round your neck.

Later on, we had two evacuee families from the east end of London. Although they had a whole floor to themselves, everyone crowded together into one room and they insisted on hanging all the baby's nappies around the cot. They rarely went out and after a few months asked to return to London. They were obviously unhappy and the countryside must have seemed alien and frightening to them.

In the summer of 1940, it was decided that we should rejoin my father in India. My sister Elizabeth, then aged twelve, remained in England,

Elizabeth in England aged twelve, 1940

living with relatives and attending boarding school. Our house in Somerset was let (we little knew that it would never be home again), and at the end of July my mother, brother and I embarked on the SS Orion, a large passenger ship of the Orient Line. However, owing to strafing by German fighters as we lay at anchor in the river Mersey, it wasn't until August that our convoy finally set sail. We headed north around the Irish coast and then west into the Atlantic. Our first destination was Cape Town before heading up into the Indian Ocean to Bombay.

After only a few days at sea, one of the Orion's propellers was damaged by enemy action, leaving us an easy prey to further attack. There was nothing for it but to return alone to port, this time to Gourock on the west coast of Scotland. We remained there for about ten days, undergoing repairs before joining another convoy, this one bound for the United States.

Out again into the Atlantic we parted from that convoy and, accompanied by an armed merchantman, swung south for the long run to Cape Town. It is only a matter of weeks ago that, quite by chance I read an obituary on the death of Michael Lethbridge, third officer on board the destroyer HMS Hurricane, and learnt the full story of the loss of City of Benares in another convoy. It had made headline news at the time, particularly because of the tragic loss of children. My eye was immediately caught by the word 'Benares' and I learnt that on 13th September 1940 the destroyer was ordered to search west of Rockall for survivors of, in fact, *two* ships from Convoy OB-213, which had been sunk by a single salvo of torpedoes from U-48. Among the complement of 406 on City of Benares were ninety children being evacuated to Canada under a plan to ship British children to safety. Hurricane picked up 105 survivors including fifteen children. A story that I have never forgotten; it could so easily have been us.

At Sierra Leone's capital, Freetown, we anchored for a day to refuel. All I remember was the heat ashore and my astonishment at seeing so many black people. It was an untidy place with tall, skinny palm trees. At sea again, this time in the exalted company of a cruiser of the Royal Dutch Navy, we at last made landfall at Table Bay and there, to our astonishment, lay the original convoy. They were equally amazed to see us, having assumed we must be at the bottom of the sea.

Cape Town was a revelation. From vast areas of dockland we drove through beautiful tree-lined streets stretching up into the hills. Everything was so clean and sparkling, each house with its gardens of brilliant flowering shrubs and swimming pool; really a paradise, and so it was – for some. Before re-embarking, we went to a small restaurant and stuffed ourselves with baked beans, sausages, bacon, eggs and much else. Ship's food did not exactly match these delicacies.

At last, on 15th September, after another long run passing Madagascar, we docked at Bombay.

2

My father was in Bombay to welcome us. Along with other families, he had spent an anxious time, since no information was available about our arrival date.

We spent a few days there, staying at the grandest hotel Colin and I had ever set eyes on. The Taj Mahal was a perfect example of the grandeur and opulence of bygone days. As it was extremely hot and we were extremely bored, we devised a cooling and amusing entertainment. Filling the bath with cold water, we soon had a mini pool and to add to the fun, sat on the back of the bath and slid down into the water, laughing and shrieking. Of course a stop was soon put to that and we sobered up considerably when later we boarded the train for a three night journey north to the Punjab and the regimental depot at Ambala.

Allenby Lines was our new address. Here on open sandy ground stood a number of pleasant red brick bungalows, situated well back from the road, each in a large and shady garden. With high ceilings and wide verandahs, the houses were both comfortable and remarkably cool. Overhead fans were installed in all the main rooms, there being no such thing as home air conditioning at that time. Personally, I infinitely prefer fans and, many years later, lived again quite happily with them in Malaysia.

From the very beginning of our arrival in India, my father insisted that we did not speak English to the house or garden staff; most did not know it anyway. My mother had long been fluent in Urdu so we two soon picked it up and being young and uninhibited, rattled along with all and sundry, especially when out on our own.

There was schooling to be considered and, although I cannot recall where Colin studied, I was sent at first to a hill station named Kasauli. There, with another girl, Jonquil Mallinson, whose father was a doctor in the Indian Army, I shared a tutor. If I learnt nothing else I did

On my hill pony, Simla 1941

acquire a love for spelling, and dictation in particular. The tutor would walk up and down behind us, reading some obscure lines and emphatically reminding us that he was only going to repeat each sentence once. Every word wrongly spelt or forgotten had to be written out several times and duly learnt.

Kasauli was like many North Indian hill stations, with its dense jungle intersected by countless broad sandy tracks. These were the roads along which rickshaws and riders travelled. Because the hillsides were very steep the roads made innumerable zigzags to reach from house to house. There was always noise from raucous birds, and the common brown monkeys in their scores jumped from tree to tree or often landed on the ground right in front of us, quite confrontational at times. Night creatures like jackals and hyenas prowled after prey. Very rarely a leopard or a bear invaded the grounds of bungalows and caused general pandemonium among the domestic animals and Indian servants.

After some months, I left Kasauli for Simla. Colin boarded there too, at the famous Mission School of Bishop Cotton. I lived with Mrs Slim, wife of General Bill Slim. He was later given command of the

14th Army in October 1943, and with it the task of expelling the Japanese from Burma.

Their daughter Una and I were the same age and together we attended Auckland House, a well known girls' school, run by an Anglican order of Grey Sisters. On our tough hill ponies, we rode the several miles to school each day and during the winter months when the Simla Club tennis courts were flooded and frozen over, we would stop off there, don our skating boots and whiz around until reminded by the syces (grooms) that we should get home. It was great fun and a relief from boring old school, for me anyway.

Born with that vivid red horseshoe mark on my forehead, I'd always loved riding and in Ambala during the holidays was allowed to exercise the old charger of one of my father's fellow officers who used to play polo. Sirdar was a beautiful chestnut gelding, standing some sixteen hands. Accompanied by the syce on his horse, we would ride out of the cantonment area and into open, scrubby country. Thin, hump backed cattle grazed and black water buffaloes wallowed lazily in the dirty, muddy pools. There were nullahs (small ditches) to be jumped and large foxholes to avoid whilst galloping over the ground.

When my father was posted elsewhere, my mother, Colin and I moved up to Simla, this time staying at the famous Cecil Hotel. Here we had the chance to explore outside the town's confines and would join friends for all day picnics in the beautiful surrounding countryside, sometimes spending a night lying out under the stars, listening to the call of the brainfever bird or the chorus of cicadas. On one of our expeditions I remember seeing a line of hill ponies and their riders moving up a rough track that seemed to fade into the rugged hills beyond. Curious, I went over to read the wording on a crude wooden signpost. It said simply, 'Tibet'.

During the hot weather season, the Viceroy always moved up to Simla and stayed at Snowdon, his regal mansion situated on a wooded hillside out of town. Once, during the Simla season, the Vicerine gave an enormous children's party. It was a very grand occasion and we not only had to dress up, but be on our best behaviour. After all, the Viceroy was the King's representative in India and had to be treated with due respect and great formality. On Sundays he and his wife attended morning service at Christ Church. Impeccably dressed, he always wore a grey frock coat and carried a matching silk top hat.

In 1942 we moved back again to Ambala, but not into a large bungalow, as before. At the far end of the cantonment some Wana huts had been erected, about which I must explain. Originally they were designed to be used in Wana, a small tribal territory on the North West Frontier. There the terrain is harsh and wild with rugged mountains and narrow gorges. The Wana huts were built of mud bricks with walls about seven feet high and roofed with canvas like a tent. Inside the hut could be divided into rooms and this is exactly how we lived for several months. For Colin and me it was a very happy time, although I did have to go unexpectedly into the military hospital one night and have my appendix speedily removed. On another occasion I was stung by a scorpion. With great presence of mind, my mother took her penknife and sliced across the top of my finger, then plastered it with grains of permanganate of potash. Our orderly predicted all sorts of dire results including death, but I survived to tell the tale.

Riding with Colonel Pop Goddard, Ambala, 1942

My father loved fishing. Whenever he could take time off we would all drive out of Ambala, through the native city and on towards the river Ghaggar. The district was called Chandi Gargh (*chandi* meaning silver and *gargh*, a place), a rural area with small farmholdings; the flat land producing maize and vegetables. I mention this because after Partition in 1947 this region of Punjab became part of India and in time a vast city was built and given the same name.

There was no bridge across the river so we drove the car onto a barge-like wooden flat and, by use of pulleys, were ferried across. My father and sometimes my mother then started the serious business of tying flies and casting their lines. Mahseer was a big fighting fish and often gave great sport, although full of bones and not much of a dish. Meanwhile, Colin and I messed around at the water's edge with our own fishing equipment – bamboo sticks with a piece of string and a worm or grub attached. These we would hopefully dangle over the bank, generally losing the bait very quickly, sadly not to a fish but just getting snagged by floating debris. It was fun and freedom to race up and down the path, checking on the parents and dying for our picnic. Halcyon days, and how fascinating and interesting they were.

Once again we all left Ambala, my father to the far south of India, there to raise and train a new battalion, and we three far north to Kashmir.

Kashmir, what memories it holds! A land of such beauty: terraced hillsides, orchards dazzling with the pink blossom of peach trees, thundering rivers, lakes and forests, but above all, the mountains. Srinagar, the capital, was built largely along both sides of the mighty Jhelum river. The houses are constructed of wood, often with attractive fretted balconies that seemed to hang right over the water. The river was the main means of transport and one took a shikara as frequently and as easily as one would a taxi. This was a slim, shallow craft, propelled by the shikara wallah using just one paddle which he switched from side to side with great dexterity. Many families lived entirely on the river, travelling like water nomads up and down in their large wooden boats known as dungas. They carried wool and very attractive woven rugs called numdahs, to be sold as they moved from place to place. They also carried their provisions, including live sheep that you could smell a long way off!

One of the greatest attractions of Srinagar was its houseboats. These artistically painted barges, well equipped with all the home comforts expected by Europeans, were rented out each summer for long or short periods, complete with cook and house boy. They were moored along the riverbank on the outskirts of the city, but also clustered at the edge of one or other of the beautiful lakes for which Kashmir is so famed. Nagin and Dal lakes offered idyllic holidays and were easily accessible for moonlight picnics or romantic evenings in the lovely Shalimar Gardens, built for the wife of the Moghul Emperor Jehangir in 1619.

For Colin and me, life was rather more down to earth. We lived across the river from Srinagar and travelled daily to school in our regular shikara. It was early spring and still extremely cold, and icicles used to form on our balaclavas well before we reached the other side.

In May of that year, 1943, the hotels and chalets opened up as usual in Gulmarg for the summer season and soon we were joining the mountain trek. Gulmarg, at 8,500 feet, was the main hill station for Srinagar. We stopped first at Tannenmarg to look at dozens of ponies and horses from which to select and hire for the season. I was lucky enough to be recommended a horse of 15 hands, called Lala. That it was one of many with the same name mattered not. Thus mounted, we began the steep ride up to Gulmarg.

Off to school on Lala, Gulmarg, 1943

My mother had rented one of the numerous wooden chalets dotted all over the hillsides and we quickly settled in. There was still school, of course, but what a difference! I now had my fine horse and once again was riding to lessons.

There were two golf courses laid out around the undulating ground rising from the small stream in a bowl of the hills. The grass was brilliant green and the scenery like Switzerland. Snow clad Mount Affarwat, at 13,600 feet, is part of the Pir Panjal Range and crouches above the resort. One of the outdoor activities considered suitable for the boys at Colin's school (Sheikh Bagh) was to climb up to a lake, break the ice and take a dip.

I attended a small school for girls, owned and run by Miss Joan Fowle (not a very fortunate name). A slight, prim lady in her fifties, she was always formally dressed, frequently in a long pleated skirt, cream blouse and cardigan. Genteel was the tone of her modest scholastic establishment. Here we learnt general subjects and particularly Latin, which Miss Fowle had read at university. I was thirteen then, a fairly lazy student, but strangely enough the Latin I acquired, or rather some of its disciplines, always remained with me. This proved very helpful when actually teaching Latin years later, but even more important when I seriously began to study the nomenclature of plants in Jordan.

We also had lessons in deportment. This always gave rise to a lot of giggling with corresponding disapproval from Miss Joan. We had to learn, amongst other things, how to sit down and rise up gracefully from an armchair or sofa. Imagine a group of awkward, plumpish teenagers lining up to try their luck at this manoeuvre! The art was to bend one knee whilst keeping the other leg straight out before lowering oneself elegantly into the sitting position – hopeless! Many a laugh I have had over those recollections.

For the riding fraternity there were drag hunts in which those with small dogs, particularly dachshunds, were set on a trail of aniseed that ran for several miles through the forest. Following your hound on horseback was great fun and, of course, many like myself went along just for the ride.

View from our chalet, Gulmarg, 1943

Homework was frequently put on the back burner, so I would arrive home in time only for a quick meal before settling down to serious study for the next day. I joined the very popular Gulmarg Pony Club and in due course learnt how to jump. Dear old Lala knew far more about it, but I still managed some falls. Once I found myself in a watery ditch, fortunately still clutching the reins and looking up at a surprised equine nose. However, perseverance paid off when together we won the Open Jumping Competition that season.

Returning briefly to Sringar, we learnt that my father was soon going overseas. He came up for a few days fishing and we camped beside the wide, fast-flowing, icy cold Lidda river, where Colin caught his first trout and my mother cut her thumb severely with a tin opener. Thankfully, the possibility of infection was stemmed by the application of many grains of permanganate of potash. This powerful disinfectant was a must in every household.

Ann and Lala, Gulmarg, 1943

So we said goodbye – forever – to Kashmir and embarked on a long, long journey south to a truly alien part of India: a place called Waltair, near Vizagapatam, on the east coast. I was not happy at Waltair. We stayed briefly in a bungalow loaned to us. I felt stifled both physically and spiritually. The heat and humidity spawned giant plants, and brilliant exotic flowers often entwined themselves amongst massive vines and creeping stems. Parrots screeched endlessly and the brainfever bird's monotonous call gave me a feeling of a lost time – time long gone, yet surrounded by the dense and somehow sinister power of rulers and nabobs who had lived in palatial mansions amidst this natural wilderness.

We soon joined my father where he was commanding his battalion in jungle camp. It was tents again, but no playing about this time, and there were strict orders to be obeyed since the area was militarily very sensitive. We spent Christmas 1943 in the jungle, Colin and I sharing a tent and learning to be quiet and not to show any lights at night. The officers held 'open house' on Christmas Day with liquor flowing generously. So generously that Colin, taking what he thought was a glass of water, quaffed it down in one, only to learn that he had mistakenly been given gin. An excellent and filling lunch seemed to soak up the worst and afterwards we all, including myself, the only girl, played a crazy game of football. It could have been a peacetime celebration, but it wasn't, and we all knew it. My father had to go to war and we had to leave India.

Lidda River, Kashmir, 1943

3

Another long train journey took us across the Eastern and Western Ghats, to arrive once more in Bombay before we set sail for England in January 1944. The fleet of ships was known as the D-Day convoy, though of course we did not know that at the time. Our huge liner was named SS Strathaird. The hundreds of troops were all confined to the lower decks and rarely allowed up top, except for exercise periods.

The ship was travelling in a wartime convoy with three sittings for each meal and all passengers assigned a particular sitting. Even if you were only minutes late, the doors were closed and that was that. With a bunch of youthful friends, we did most things together, including eating. As well as Colin and myself, my mother had agreed to escort a small boy back to England to join his grandparents and live with them until the end of the war. We had been given a single cabin for the four of us with an added extra bunk. So my mother took the upper one, Colin and Christopher shared the lower one and I had a mattress on the floor. Thus we travelled for some two months. I don't believe we had a porthole, and it wouldn't have made any difference since there was permanent and total blackout throughout the voyage.

With so much spare time and literally nowhere to go, the youngsters had nothing to do. Soon enough, however, some enterprising men and women appeared out of the woodwork to offer their services and expertise in such subjects as geology, Morse code, mathematics and astronomy. There were theorists in this and that, which just added to the flavour of our studies, but made little lasting impression. Lessons were held deep down in the ship where electric light was always needed and I'm sure many mothers suffered real anxiety on our account.

So we sailed, not round the Cape again, but across the Indian Ocean, up the Red Sea to berth at Port Tewfiq, not far from Suez. One of the ships was in need of repair, so all passengers and soldiery of the convoy were disembarked and sent to tented camps, women and children together, the soldiers elsewhere near the Suez Canal. Our camp was surrounded by high wire fencing, with Italian prisoners of war engaged to keep the place running and to cook, Egyptian guards and a WRAC (Women's Royal Army Corps) sergeant in charge – quite a setup. We ate in Nissen huts, and I chiefly remember porridge full of weevils, and tea, milk and sugar served together in huge teapots – and yams. I've disliked yams ever since.

There was adventure too, for some. One day a youngster reported seeing horses outside the camp so we raced out to look. Sure enough, several animals were being exercised nearby and presently there were invitations to have a ride. I was soon mounted and when the groom saw that I could manage he allowed me to go for a short circuit alone. Alas, the second time round my horse just took the bit between its teeth and before I knew what was happening we were away, jumping two railway lines, up a steep embankment, across the main Suez-Cairo trunk road and down the other side. I remember thinking seriously of trying to fall off, but in the end just clung on, sawing uselessly at the bit in a vain attempt to stop the animal. By now we were amongst the soldiers' tents and getting very close to the water of the canal. At last, when I felt sure it would break its leg amongst the tent ropes, the exhausted beast stopped. I couldn't move but just sat like a rag doll and cried. The horrified groom eventually arrived and led me back to camp. There was quite a reception and my mother, to cover her extreme worry, expended some wrath on me.

That was only one adventure. More were to follow. Some days later Christopher went down with chickenpox and was put into isolation at the 13th General Hospital up the road. Then, together with Colin, a Mrs Morris and me, my mother decided to take a day trip to Cairo. Picture a black line running through miles and miles of dirty yellow sand. That was our road to the 'bright lights' of Cairo. Of course, there was no public transport – remember we were at war – so we split up: Colin with my mother, me with Mrs Morris. A British Army truck soon picked them up, and eventually we two climbed up into the cab of a heavily laden fuel tanker driven by a very large, very jolly black driver. Whilst the others sailed gaily on towards Cairo, in no time at all our man was stopped and we were ignominiously made to get down. Two females in a fuel tanker driven by a black man was more than the authorities would permit. So once again we waited hopefully and in due course made it to Cairo. By a miraculous chance we all met up at the same YWCA, not realizing that several existed in the city. First stop was at Groppi's, the internationally renowned patisserie. There, with our eyes far bigger than our stomachs – remember the camp food – we chose the largest, creamiest confections, and even Colin, who always had a passion for meringues, was quite unable to cope. We did not know what was to follow. Nothing daunted, however, we progressed out to the pyramids and then to the famous Mina House Hotel for lunch. By this time Colin was looking distinctly yellow and feeling very sick. It was time to head back to the 'delights' of tented Tewfiq. We took a train, but on reaching our supposed destination were informed that there was an epidemic of bubonic plague and urged to continue to the next station where a military ambulance met and swiftly conveyed us back to camp. There was no plague infection, but Colin had joined the chickenpox brigade and was whisked up to join Christopher at the hospital.

All these excitements had occurred over a three week period and very soon it was time to re-embark again. By now I, too, had begun to show telltale spots, and the four of us, together with one or two other similarly afflicted families, were put on a hospital ferry and taken straight to the ship's hospital. My mother and both boys were allowed back to their cabin; I spent two miserable weeks in a hospital bed until no longer contagious. As the only youngster amongst really sick adults, it was not a pleasant experience. There was nothing to do and always that ghastly blue light shining in one's eyes, day and night.

However, there was one bright spot. Somehow, it became known that I was about to celebrate my fourteenth birthday and the chef presented me with an absolutely scrumptious chocolate cake. I recall the taste, even now; the chocolate butter filling was really something.

Once through the canal, we set sail into the Mediterranean and each ship now carried a huge barrage balloon. Its role was to make it difficult for low-flying enemy aircraft to fire at or bomb their targets accurately. Here we ran into a series of exceptionally violent winter storms. Deep, rumbling thunder rolled across livid skies with brilliant lightning etching the ships as they wallowed and tossed in mountainous seas. Our only escort was the pocket battleship, HMS Warspite, and many times she seemed to disappear completely beneath the waves. Needless to say, all balloons were lost.

So we sailed on, with even more rigorous orders about showing any light. Torches or the glow of a cigarette were absolutely forbidden anywhere on or near the open decks. The Germans had received word that a very large convoy was moving through the Med at that time, but did not know its direction. Very soon all the ships began a constant pattern of zigzagging. Not finding us, the German aircraft turned east in their search, and so we passed through the Straits of Gibraltar, round Portugal by Cape St Vincent and up north into the Bay of Biscay. Finally, towards the end of March, the convoy came to anchor in the Firth of Clyde.

Standing on an upper deck I looked across the water to beautiful snow covered hills, their purple peaks etched against a winter sky, beautiful, but alien. My thoughts were far away amongst other ancient beautiful hills in a land I loved and have always loved. There was one very personal farewell to make. My topi (pith helmet) had been with me throughout the three and a half years I had spent in India. We had shared so many rides, so many adventures. I could not let it come to a foreign land. Standing at the rail, with falling tears, I flung it as far as I could into the water. To this day, the remembrance brings sadness. It was a farewell to so much that lay in my heart.

Following disembarkation, trains had been commandeered for the women and children, and all through the night we sped south, sitting or standing in icy carriages. Soldiers brought us food packs and everything seemed so strange and foreign. Christopher's grandparents collected him in London and we three went to my grandmother's house in Newbury.

4

Very soon Colin was at school in north Devon and I joined my sister at Downe House outside Newbury. Elizabeth left almost immediately to join the WRNS (Women's Royal Naval Service) and I lived outside the school that summer term of 1944. With another girl, I shared a room in a charming house belonging to the domestic science teacher. It was a ten minute walk to school through dense woodland. Although by the second term I was boarding in the school, the woods, dark and dripping, always gave me a sense of menace.

For someone brought up from an early age to be self-reliant, I found the many petty rules irksome. A matron to supervise your hair washing and nail cutting was an insult. Throughout the school, winter and summer, when the rising bell went, one and all had to strip off their nightwear and plunge into a cold bath. The idea was probably to invigorate body and mind for the day ahead. Anyway, by Christmas of that year I was still suffering from a chronic bladder infection I had contracted in India. So, thankfully, I left Downe and, after a term studying at home, went to St Swithun's outside Winchester. What a difference: individual houses, no cold baths and plenty of sport. We had a lovely garden and a tennis court.

That was the summer I was nearly expelled. Each weekend there was house swimming – without compulsory lengths or certain strokes, so of course we had fun. Such fun that one warm afternoon after being told, 'Time's up, out you get,' Miss Warne, the mistress in charge, left for her car. A very bright spark, Colleen Vaughan, dared those of us already in the changing cubicles to come out just as we were and jump into the pool again. It so happened that most of us were in the altogether, but nothing daunted, we jumped straight back into the water shrieking and laughing. Of course this brought the swift return of Miss Warne and next day found us, one by one, in front of the headmistress, Miss Watt. I cannot imagine Miss Watt ever contemplating doing something so outrageous, and she was shocked beyond measure. In the event no one was expelled; a misdemeanour of little significance. I left school in 1947 and, being interested in the growing and marketing of garden crops, I went to work for a local market gardener near home in order to gain practical experience before starting serious study at the Devon Farm Institute.

That summer was a watershed for my father who had only recently left India for good, following Partition. Twenty seven years' service in the Indian Army could not be easily shrugged off. No longer young, what was he to do? For a while he worked with the Civil Defence covering a large area of Devon, where we now lived.

By 1953 we had moved again, this time near Winchester. Father had always been most interested in history and historical events. He was meticulous in his research and an excellent and informed speaker. He soon became very knowledgeable about Winchester, Salisbury and the New Forest, and in that Coronation year, offered his services as a guide to one of the local travel agents. In our small family car he took numbers of visitors around and soon built up a fine reputation.

My parents and Elizabeth had attended the coronation of King George VI and Queen Elizabeth in 1937. This time my father and I journeyed to London for the crowning of their daughter. We had seats in Hyde Park and had to be there by seven o'clock in the morning. It was a very long wait with drizzle on and off most of the day, but stuffing sheets of newspaper down our backs kept the damp and the wind at bay. We were thrilled to learn, maybe even before Her Majesty, that Edmund Hillary and Tenzing Norgay had conquered Mount Everest. Finally, at around three o'clock, the cheers reached a crescendo as Queen Elizabeth II, together with Prince Philip, passed slowly by in the glittering State Coach.

All that summer my father kept busy but my mother knew that there must be a continuation, and she encouraged him to go to London and qualify as a member of the Guild of Guide Lecturers. So that is what he did, and at the age of fifty seven he became a student, attending lectures and spending many hours on his own, simply walking the streets of London and familiarizing himself with its vast history. Having qualified, he further increased his knowledge of other interesting places, building up a series of attractive itineraries. At first he was employed by the large London agents, but later, as more and more people wanted personal guiding, he became very well known, especially amongst wealthy, cultured Americans, many of whom had their roots in British society.

Back to earth, I was moving around in the gardening world and gaining both knowledge and expertise in the field of cut flowers. I spent some time at a place in Hampshire, which taught me a lot, but where the millionaire employer had little regard or consideration for his staff. His only child, a girl of about nine, would come into the gardens bringing her two corgis. She knew that dogs were strictly forbidden in the marketing area, but seemed to take pleasure in letting them chase each other over delicate plants. When we tried to catch them they just bit us.

I became engaged and later disengaged between the spring and autumn of 1953. My fiancé, who was stationed in Germany that summer, was quite badly hurt when his light aircraft crashed in woods, just a few weeks before our wedding. Everything was put on hold, but when John returned to England he was a changed man. I eventually learnt that while in Germany, he had taken a fancy to the sister of a brother officer. And so it ended.

I needed to get away from home, away from England, and accepted a short term offer to fly out to Turkey as a nanny/help with a Diplomatic family.

5

New Year's Eve 1953 found me in Istanbul. My employers lived across the Bosphorus in Asia Minor, in a neighbourhood called Moda. My new address was 25 Mektep Sokak (School Street), in one of the many old style Turkish houses. They were tall and narrow with only two or three rooms to each floor, so one always seemed to be going either up or down. With two small boys and a baby to care for, I was kept pretty busy. Nicolas and Charlie attended a little private school a few streets away, and I'll never forget the icy winds and the snow while walking with them during those winter months. Ships were locked into the frozen Bosphorus. But spring arrived eventually and with it the flowers. Mount Aidos, about an hour away from Moda, was a sea of wild anemones, scarlet, mauve and white. I had never seen anything like it and was quite dazzled. Dozens of other spring flora appeared, whose names, alas, I did not know at that time, and tortoises were everywhere, knocking shells with a fancied female. How beautiful it all was, and the sea never far away.

Several interesting people lived in Mektep Sokak. Some were of old Yorkshire stock, whose grandfathers had left England's shores to find fortune in the Levant during the mid-nineteenth century. Turkey had long been a great trading centre and, together with its commerce and banking interests, was a challenge and an adventure for the hard headed, down-to-earth north countrymen. The Whittall family in particular prospered exceedingly. The earliest Whittall, newly married, sailed with his bride and all his chattels for the Sublime Porte around the late 1840s. There he met many entrepreneurs and adventurers, amongst them Greeks and Armenians. Business relationships were established and soon the increasingly wealthy newcomers were building their mansions. They chose to live on the Asian side, and I visited one or two around Moda and later in Izmir (or Smyrna as it was originally known). Within the airy rooms, the high walls were often decorated with beautiful ceramic tiles. Handsome, heavy, old-fashioned furniture filled most of the space, and always there was a samovar. On those winter evenings we loved sitting round the table, our knees and legs warm beneath the long chenille cloth. In summertime tea was taken in the garden – so English, with its flower-filled borders, perfect lawn and in the centre a mulberry tree, arched and graceful, the branches touching the ground.

The La Fontaines and the Girauds were Huguenot families, originally from France, who had established themselves very successfully in Izmir. With Christians in the minority and few of them Protestants, it was not surprising that the three families soon intermarried, building up a formidable hierarchy. Sons followed their fathers and took wives from amongst their kith and kin, one or two bringing home a 'foreign' bride. Listening to their stories made me think of The Forsyte Saga. Looking back on those days of the 1950s, I realize I was witnessing the closing of an era. Sometimes I would arrange to meet Kenny Whittall, (the doyen of the family) for lunch, and waiting for him in his Istanbul office down near the Galata Bridge beside the Golden Horn, I would listen to him switching effortlessly between English, Greek and Turkish as the situation demanded. Excitement and tension pulsed through those warehouses and banking centres.

* * * * *

Before the weather became too hot I joined three friends exploring lesser known parts of Turkey. In an ancient Land Rover we travelled first to Ankara, stopping overnight before beginning the really interesting journey.

Moving south we headed towards Ürgüp, skirting the enormous Tuz Golu (salt lake), a sheet of dazzling turquoise. We found the village more by chance than good navigation after driving some distance along a beautiful watered valley. The whole district was abundant with vegetables: green beans, spring onions in perfect rows, sweet red peppers, aubergines, and great patches of sunflowers. At the end lay the village, simple two storied dwellings with open verandahs and balconies, and steps leading down to the street. There being no hotel accommodation the village elder assigned us a single room above the communal potato store and reached by a rickety wooden ladder. The iron bedsteads were well padded with sheepskins (surprisingly sweet smelling) and for coverings we had the black and white skins of the Zakko goat.

The following day we spent exploring this remarkable troglodyte valley. Entering the fifth-century churches, which had been carved into the rocks, one's breath was taken away by the beautiful frescoes which decorated them. The domes and walls depicted many biblical scenes and because little sunlight penetrated the churches the colours were amazingly fresh and vibrant.

There was interest too in the village itself. The lokanta, or meeting eating place, was rather like a country pub. The simple wooden bar was stocked with raki, vodka, beer and a local wine. Men sat at small tables or lounged on benches along the walls, puffing at their handmade clay pipes. But the most fascinating figure was a woman. Far from her first youth and ugly to boot, she nevertheless held complete sway in that smoke-filled room. She too smoked, and she talked. This was her story: Years before as a village bride, she and her husband had lived together with her mother-in-law and another woman. This other woman was deemed 'simple' and had always been treated as a maid. Time went by, the family increased and all was harmonious, until one day, the husband took this maid to wife. Our friend, as she told us, was outraged and for many weeks remonstrated with him, to no avail, until one day she upped and killed him with an axe.

She was tried, found guilty and in due course of law imprisoned for seventeen years. When we met her she had just been released. So we had the story straight from the horse's mouth, so to speak. Prison appeared to have done little to dampen her spirits and, if anything, only added to her prestige.

We left Ürgüp reluctantly and spent several boring hours on a long, dull stretch of plain heading for Konya. This large agricultural centre was of little interest, though the town had once housed an ancient, religious order, founded by Mevlana, a thirteenth-century Sufi mystic. At one time it was the spiritual home of the Dervishes, a sect of Sufism. Here one could watch their famous whirling dances, performed by men and boys. In long white pleated robes tied at the waist with wide sashes, and wearing the famous red conical hats, they circled endlessly around as the drumbeat intensified and the figures began to merge as one.

From now on we travelled through magnificent scenery, crossing the Taurus Mountains and meeting many migrating nomads. The Ürüks in particular are a gypsy people. At one stage, on the steep zigzag road, we encountered an entire tribe. Flocks of sheep and goats swarmed up the hillsides, the sound of their bells echoing in the pure air as they grazed the lush new grass. Heavily laden camels swayed beneath vast bundles of firewood and great pots and pans which jangled against their flanks. Often a woman was atop, suckling her infant or clutching a young child. I was very struck by the beauty of the women and girls. Totally unveiled and attired in vibrant shades of purple, pink and green, many of them wore headbands of gold and silver coins.

They were moving up to the rich summer pastures, a gay, lively, uninhibited people, so at home in their world and full of life and laughter. I always wished we had met more of them.

It was May and getting hotter each day as we moved south towards the Mediterranean coast. The small fishing town of Alanya was our next destination and, if I close my eyes now, I can still see the dazzling light on the water and the high rocky headland above the port, silhouetted against a crimson sky. Everything was so green and alive, orange trees in bloom giving that strangely sweet scent of tropical growth.

The first evening, after a careful search, we settled on a 'newly opened' *oteli*. Built of wood and pretty basic, the proprietor, however, was pleasant and helpful and directed us to the best *lokanta*. We had to walk along a narrow, ill-lit lane, but the meal certainly came up to its billing: beans, pilaf, kebab and of course dolmas (vine leaves filled with minced lamb and savoury rice), hunks of bread and a local wine.

One of us wanted to smoke so, having finished eating, I offered to return to the hotel for the cigarettes. So far so good, but on my return, I could hear footsteps following very close behind me. When I stopped, they stopped. Scared to turn round and confront my shadow, I nervously continued walking back to the *lokanta*. What a relief when I arrived! But those same footsteps were now inside, and imagine my astonishment when I discovered that they belonged to the son of the restaurateur, who had been bidden to accompany the 'foreign' lady to and from her destination. What kindness and graciousness!

We sortied from Alanya, along the coast, first to Side. A vast Graeco-Roman city had once dominated this spot. Though much of the stone and marble had been pillaged over the centuries, the ruins were impressive and we all enjoyed sitting astride an intricately carved and partially submerged column, dabbling our feet in the warm water, like being in a Turkish bath but at no cost. Later on we explored Aspendos, also Graeco-Roman, but here there was only the theatre. The atmosphere was quite different; sombreness and a strange silence pervaded. The individual building stones were enormous, three foot by four at least. I saw a chameleon for the first time and was fascinated by its colour changes. We actually picked one off a twig and placed it among some leaves, where it duly became green.

The story of these great cities is similar to so many throughout the Near East. It was savaged by foreign attacks and invasions – in this case by the Seljuks, marauding and destroying as they passed – and finally massive earthquakes toppled most of what still stood intact.

Our next stop was the present day popular resort of Antalya. Around sixty years ago it was just a charming seaside town with a small harbour. The river did not flow into the sea in the usual manner, but hurled itself in a thunderous roar over the cliffs. These were the Düden Falls. Together with the powerful spray and baking sun, we all got badly burned. We had intended to spend that night in Denizli, but did not make it and opted instead for Budur. There was nothing special here, but it seems we created quite a stir. Foreigners were a rare sight in this railway town and before we had been ten minutes in the place a student appeared and took us on a tour. This had to include the station and an engine, a sugar factory, the lycée, and a stop to admire some fine furniture making with designs from a 1936 catalogue. Last but not least, the girls of our group attended a bride's wedding preparations. By the end of the evening I don't know which of us was the most tired.

Returning to Denizli the following day in brilliant sunshine, we explored the world famous 'petrified terraces' of Pamukkale ('cotton castle' in Turkish). The terraces are formed by a consistent build up of calcium carbonate. Pools the colour of opal and pale jade descended the hillside, each encrusted in dazzling white. I have never seen anything like this, before or since.

It was a long run up through Bursa and Izmit until we made landfall at Moda. That very special trip was in 1954. The southern coast of Turkey has now become a tourist playground, and I am sure I would no longer recognise the once beautiful and remote region.

* * * * *

The history of old Istanbul and its fabulous architecture is a never-ending source of interest and fascination. Crossing the Golden Horn by the Galata Bridge is like stepping back into history. The magnificence of Aya Sophia, and the Sultan Ahmed Mosque (unique with six minarets), the Seraglio Palace, the Byzantine churches and the old defensive walls all speak of the conquest and glorification of the city.

There was old world charm to be found on the Princes' Islands, a small archipelago lying in the Sea of Marmara, just off the Asian shore. Motor traffic was banned throughout. Just the clip clop of hooves could be heard as horses pulled the wooden phaetons along quiet country roads. Many Greeks and Armenians spent the summer months on the islands, commuting daily to Istanbul by ferry. They were oases of peace when I knew them all those years ago.

In August of the same year I left Turkey with my employers. We took ship, passing Greece through the Corinth Canal, to disembark at Venice. There was little time to explore the city except to visit St

Mark's Cathedral and the Doge's Palace – no standing on the Bridge of Sighs or travelling in a gondola! By train we sped across Europe and so to England. There I said my goodbyes and within six weeks was again on my travels.

6

To faraway places I was certainly heading, this time engaged as tutor to two small boys. It was a challenging assignment since I had never taught in my life. The parents, Brigadier and Mrs Harris, appeared confident in my capabilities, and so it was that October 1954 found me setting sail alone for Malaya and Penang. It was a fun voyage with nothing to do but enjoy myself. I became passionate about table tennis and deck tennis, entering every possible competition and becoming notorious at sending the quoits overboard. I did pick up a few trophies, though.

The ship, the SS Chusan, the newest and largest of the P&O liners, called at Colombo where we were able to go ashore for a day. I opted for the zoo and rode on a giant tortoise. The voyage continued, and from then on it was a steady passage until we anchored in Penang. As we manoeuvred to the dockside, the first things that caught my eye were hundreds of large jellyfish. The sea was thick with them. They looked like huge floating egg yolks, attached to many long white threads. Once ashore, my new boss and his wife took me off to their hotel to have lunch and to meet Cecil, aged seven, and Armor, five. You can imagine it was a rather strained first encounter. I was tired and overexcited and only too aware of how I was being sized up.

The next day we left the island and drove many miles south to Ipoh. I was fascinated by everything: the jungle density mile after mile, acres of brilliant green *padi*, houses built on stilts, and just the colour and smell. Ipoh was the headquarters of the Brigade that Tommy Harris was commanding, although most of the troops were serving further north in the jungle. The reason for all this military action throughout Malaya was the insurgence of Communist terrorists, recruited mainly from China. Known as the Emergency, it was a murderous and long drawn out campaign, costing many lives and lasting several years. The managers of rubber plantations were greatly at risk. Most lived alone, running vast estates. Miles off the road, they were frequently ambushed, often wounded or killed.

Ipoh, the capital of the state of Perak, was similar in many ways to an Indian cantonment. The houses were often two storied, large and comfortable. Gardens were a dazzle of colour with exotic plants flowering year round, there being little change in temperature, except during the monsoon season. Most days we had heavy but brief showers, always hoping they would not interfere too much with afternoon games of tennis or golf.

Before moving into 1 Racecourse Road, we stayed first in a Chinese hotel called the Ruby Boarding House. Here I started lessons with Cecil and Armor. My bedroom with a large dressing table and two chairs served as our first schoolroom. It was a very difficult and testing time. After two weeks I had become most disheartened and discouraged. What was I doing in a situation like this? But there was no going back, and as the days passed I suddenly began to see light, both for the boys and myself. By the time we had settled comfortably into Racecourse Road a short while later, I realized with amazement that I had begun a love affair with teaching. It has remained with me ever since.

Ipoh was a great place. The town was attractively laid out and everything was green and colourful. Gardeners vied with one another to produce the most spectacular displays for their *tuan* (sirs). Many houses had their own tennis court and swimming pool. I joined the Tennis Club where one could make up a four most afternoons. The Ipoh Club, too, was extremely well appointed and set in lovely grounds. A somewhat robust form of Scottish dancing took place weekly, and on several occasions I found myself pushed into the swimming pool by my over enthusiastic dancing partner.

Throughout my two and a quarter years in Malaya, I tried to see as much of the country as possible. This was not too easy with so much fighting, but as well as several trips to stay with friends in Kuala Lumpur, I have memories of a wonderful long weekend spent on the east coast. Flying over dense jungle from Ipoh to Kota Baharu, I took a taxi south, down the coastal road, and several hours later arrived at the charming fishing village of Kota Terengganu. There I put up at the State rest house which was right by the sea. I could have jumped out of the bedroom window straight onto perfect golden sand stretching for miles along the palm fringed shore.

The people here were not Malays, but Chinese. They had most probably migrated from China years before, converted to Islam and entirely adapted themselves to the traditional ways of the region, making a reasonable livelihood by fishing, weaving and working with silver. Reached by ladders, all the simple wooden houses stood on stilts, thus protected during the monsoon season, with its frequent devastating rains, especially near the coast.

As the only European I attracted a fair amount of attention, but soon broke the ice amongst the youngsters by teaching them how to play noughts and crosses. After swimming or racing along the beach, a group of boys and girls would cluster round me and watch with giggles as I drew huge criss crossed lines on the sand. By dint of some Malay and sign language, they soon cottoned on and competition became fierce. By the time I finally gave up there was an endless trail of scratches to mark the keen progress I had inadvertently instigated.

During one summer leave I opted to go to Hong Kong, sailing from Singapore to Kowloon on the Lloyd Triestino Line. Not having much money, I had bought a ticket which allowed me to sleep on board. It was August and steaming hot with no cooling off at night; being by the water made it much worse.

I did all the usual tourist things like taking the funicular up the Peak, enjoying Stanley Gardens and, of course, making frequent ferry crossings to mainland Kowloon and the fleshpots of shopping. I found a pretty set of silver teaspoons with jade tops for my mother; she left them back to me and I have them here in Amman more than fifty years on. Chinese silk kimonos were a 'best buy', cheap and lasting forever. Views from the island were spectacular if not always beautiful. The incredibly tall waterfront blocks were dazzling with the sun on their sheets of glass windows, but I loved watching the massive, seemingly cumbersome junks as they manoeuvred between the island and the mainland. Like twentieth-century Spanish galleons, they were often festooned with flags and huge red banners portraying dragons. Their main port was Aberdeen and there they hunkered down in hundreds, floating amidst appalling squalor. Everything went overboard, from refuse to rats. It was a truly terrible waterway, the smell assailing your nostrils long before you arrived. Three days later I was heading back to Singapore.

As the heat and humidity rose, the Harrises rented a bungalow in a small hill station above Ipoh called Maxwell Hill. Driving up and round literally dozens of hairpin bends, we eventually came out above the jungle line and into another world. There were charming wooden bungalows with wide verandahs and incredible views. Deciduous trees and shrubs grew amongst English flowers. It was warm during the day, but in the evening we needed a wood fire and blankets on the beds. Tracks took one everywhere and I came across butterflies and moths of immense size and beauty. When it rained the air was sharp and fresh and the wind blew cool on your face. We had several short breaks like this and I always thought how wise it was.

In 1955 we moved further north to Taiping, which in Chinese means "great peace". I was very sorry to leave Ipoh and my friends, but soon discovered just how charming was Taiping, a much smaller town with hills around and the municipal gardens in the centre. There, the golf course was laid out amidst the greenest of grass, lovely flowerbeds and beautiful fan palms. Above the golf course stood the Taiping Club with its tennis courts and attractive clubhouse. Nearby was the Anglican church and, not far away, the prison. I used to walk past the latter every day on my way home after tennis, often receiving wolf whistles from the inmates.

The Harrises had a really fine house in Taiping and I cherished every minute of my time. Whenever I smell the scent of frangipani I'm reminded vividly of the lovely trees in our garden. I drew a pastel of the cream flowers set against their dark green foliage.

There were few single females and so one was invited out a good bit. With only the cinema as the outside attraction, entertaining was done almost entirely at home. As all houses were well staffed it was easy to get up a party at short notice. We did Scottish dancing or played charades, but most often just enjoyed sitting together in good company, with a long drink and listening to the old fashioned record player.

There was, however, one exception. A certain bachelor planter enjoyed some wilder fun. This involved shooting corks and bottle tops off the window ledges. You took the rifle and, resting the barrel on the back of the sofa at the far end of the room, took aim and hoped to hit the target. Many shots went wide and disappeared into the darkness. I always prayed that no one was walking underneath.

The two main sources of income throughout Malaya were rubber planting and tin mining. Rubber trees were grown on a vast scale and Tamils from South India were employed in the care and daily tapping of the trees. Early morning, generally before sunrise, the tappers were at work. An incision of some inches was made along the bark of each tree and a small metal cup hung below to catch the white latex. At the end of the day all the latex was collected into large containers and, in due course, sent to the factory for cleaning, washing and rolling. The huge white sheets were then transferred to hang on racks in the wooden drying sheds. A slow-burning fire gradually turned them brown and the smell was just like cooking kippers.

Tin mining was open cast and worked mostly in the northern state of Kedah where the hills are higher and pretty rugged. Like other forms of mining, the large pieces of rock were graded, broken down and washed to expose the mineral. It was a very lucrative industry, but the demand for tin began to fall, being replaced in many cases by silicones and plastics, and in the end the industry was unable to compete profitably on the open market.

My next adventure outside Malaya was a train journey to Bangkok. Just like the proverbial 'slow boat to China', it seemed to take forever. In fact, it was two nights and three stifling days, the train rarely seeming to exceed a walking pace. We stopped to pick up women off to market or children off to school, and often for no reason at all. There was of course no air conditioning, and in April temperatures were building up a good head of heat and humidity. I shared a four berth compartment with a missionary lady from Penang and we pooled our food and, more importantly, drink. Water was never safe taken from a tap or at a station unless bottled by some recognized company.

In Bangkok I spent the first night or two at the American Presbyterian Mission House, which was a B&B. Their breakfast was a fun meal and, for me, novel. As well as fresh fruit such as papaya, lychees and bananas, there was always a main course. This ranged from pork chops or waffles, to scrambled eggs with marmalade. Later I moved into the chummery of the British Embassy, where the single girls were housed.

After Taiping, Bangkok was vast, and with only limited funds I did a great deal of walking. Once I braved a tram ride and then got off far too soon for fear of being taken into the unknown. There were so many temples, one really had to be selective, and all I saw were impressive. I liked walking along the length of the recumbent Buddhas and trying to picture how they had been made. I always regretted that I had neither time nor money to travel north to the great teak forests of Chiang Mai and see the elephants. There was anything and everything to tempt the visitor, chief of which was the famous and beautiful Thai silk. I'm mad about colour, so it wasn't difficult to be tempted inside dozens of material shops. I kept my purchases down to a scarf, lengths of blue and sea green silk, and then fled.

A boat trip was also a must and, though the wide, fast flowing Chao Phraya was extremely polluted, the pretty girls selling their exotic blooms or colourful fruits from small river craft, and the tea houses and cafés jutting out above the water were certainly picturesque.

On one occasion I was invited to an evening of Scottish dancing followed by supper. Sometime after midnight I was dropped at the entrance to my bungalow and started walking in near darkness along the driveway. Suddenly, I felt a very sharp needle-like stab in my big toe. I hurried on to the house to look at the damage and consult with the night watchman. No help there, and by the time I reached my room the toe was red and swelling. I shall never forget that trauma. Everyone was asleep and I was by now quite sure I had been bitten by a venomous snake. I wriggled my toes and found my foot had become much stiffer. I just sat on the bed, rigid with fear, saying goodbye to all my family. Eventually, completely worn out by the terrible stress, I fell asleep, fully clothed. A sharp flint must have caught my bare foot, but it could so well have been a snake. Ironically, I had that day been to watch dozens of the writhing creatures being fed at the famous Pasteur Institute.

* * * * *

In 1956 the Harris family was on the move again, this time much further south, to Malacca. My paternal grandfather had worked with the Survey Department throughout the Straits Settlements, as they were then known, and he would have been very familiar with the town of Malacca. It has a colonial history starting with the arrival of the Portuguese in 1511, who in turn were driven out by the Dutch. There is a small rise above the town, and on it stands the ruins of St Paul's, a sixteenth-century church, together with a separate bell tower, which served as a lighthouse. I was interested to see how the gravestones within the ruins had been put to use twice, in many cases with both Dutch and Portuguese inscriptions. Down by the sea stands what was the Stadthuys (governor's house) and the law court, built in terracotta stone in 1650.

We lived some miles out of town, with neighbours few and far between. I was not very happy there, but it was the last six months of my employment.

I left the Harrises in November 1956 and travelled by train to board a ship at Singapore. Both Tommy and AnneMarie came to see me off. I was really surprised to find myself in a long compartment with bunks either side and Chinese families preparing their food on the floor. AnneMarie helped me to stow my baggage, but made no comment whatsoever about the accommodation – very strange. Were they cost-cutting or did they feel that was my place? There was absolutely no privacy and I undressed sitting on my lower bunk, literally cheek by jowl with my Chinese fellow travellers, men and women.

It was the time of the Suez Crisis and once again I made the sailing around the Cape of Good Hope. The SS Canton was a much smaller sister ship of the Chusan in which I had travelled out to Malaya, but great fun nonetheless. Sixteen years on, I saw again the majestic sight of Table Mountain and Cape Town. We had a whole day in which to explore something of the city and enjoy the spectacular views of both Indian and Atlantic oceans. Cape Town had grown beyond belief and was as attractive as I remembered it from all those years back. We visited the vineyards at Stellenbosch, and the museum so associated with the life of General Smuts. During these excursions I became acutely aware of the racial segregation – no coloured people allowed on buses for whites.

7

I arrived back in England on 24th December 1956, just in time for a family Christmas. It was years since Elizabeth, Colin and I had been together with our parents. Elizabeth had been living and working in Canada since 1951 and this was her first visit back. On 15th January she was married to David Chester at the Charterhouse Chapel in the city of London. My godfather, Canon John Campbell, who was the Master of Charterhouse, conducted the service.

After all the festivities Colin then elected to have his appendix removed and I began the serious business of looking for work – in England.

With two plus years' experience behind me and an excellent reference from the preparatory school that Cecil joined at the beginning of 1957, I settled into a fine private pre-prep school in Wetherby Gardens, just off Earl's Court Road. It was owned by Gerald and Margaret Russell, Margaret running the teaching side and Gerald the administration.

During my interview with Margaret I told her that I had no degree, nor had I ever taught in a school. I left the meeting not very optimistic. Imagine my surprise and astonishment when I was offered the post of teacher to a small class of six to seven year olds. It was a very fine place and I learnt a tremendous amount. Sadly, I only stayed eighteen months as I couldn't save anything on a salary of £8 a week. But I never lost contact with the Russells and when I married in 1964 they attended my wedding.

The next teaching assignment was very different: a saga of sorrows and tragic happenings. In December 1958 I met an Anglo-Swiss family in London who wanted a private tutor for their seven-year-old son. They lived in Switzerland, some distance from Zurich. I accepted to fly out early in January and duly made my arrangements.

While I was literally waiting to board the plane for Zurich, a telephone call came through. Mr Matter, my employer, was on the line and told me that his little daughter, Wheelan, had been drowned in her bath. I was absolutely shocked and asked if he would like me to postpone or cancel my journey. He insisted on my travelling out as arranged and duly met me at the airport, with a very sleepy small son. On the way to Au, where they lived, he apologized for his wife's absence. 'I am sorry my wife is not here to meet you; she's in prison,' were his very words. So in this incredible manner did I begin a job that would become more and more macabre and tragic.

The large chalet owned by the Matters was high above Lake Zurich and, as I first saw it, hidden in deep snow. It was a grim arrival and I felt lost and totally disorientated by these events. Wheelan's funeral took place two days later for which her mother was allowed out of gaol. I had the task of trying to explain to Timothy why his sister was being buried and why his parents had not taken him to her burial.

The funeral over and few visitors to call and condole, Buddy Matter was released from prison, came home and shut herself up. She refused to see Timothy. I rarely saw her, and then only to note her extreme thinness and the empty whisky bottles lying on the floor of that shuttered room. I settled down to teach Timothy, and Rolf (Mr Matter) left for his work in Zurich.

The house was a large three storied chalet and the two young Italian maids continued to cook and clean, but there was no family life, and I soon discovered what an extremely tough and difficult child Timothy was. My room was on the top floor. The best part of it was the balcony, from which I looked out over fields and woods rising into the snow-clad hills. I painted the walls of the room and put up some pretty curtains and, with my own personal belongings, gradually made it homelike. It became a real sanctuary as the months went by and the domestic situation deteriorated on all fronts. I struggled with Timothy who simply didn't intend to learn. Just before lessons he would often run out of the house and hide somewhere, not answering any calls. Half an hour later he would turn up and sit sulkily at his desk as I tried to instill some knowledge into him. I soon grew to dread our scholastic sessions as, besides having a strong aversion to study, Timothy had a violent temper and most aggressive manner. He was physically very strong and I simply couldn't hold him as he fought to get out of the room.

So matters continued. The estrangement between husband and wife widened into a gulf of bitterness and recriminations. Rolf Matter took to staying away from the house until late at night and Buddy continued with the bottle. I gradually learnt more about the probable causes of the marital breakdown. Buddy was English, the daughter of a very wealthy self-made tycoon. After her marriage, she had bought Rolf a share in a lucrative Swiss firm importing petroleum from Romania. That put him in a weak position from the start and she made sure he knew it. It seems that mama-in-law was the proverbial interfering type, although she lived in Berne. Constantly telephoning to ask about the children and apparently not satisfied with the answers, she employed a private detective to spy around the premises. To counter these insistent calls the Matters closed the telephone lines. When tragedy struck and little Wheelan was drowned, there was no phone to call for help.

Occasionally the Matter parents would go off to Zurich for the day on a shopping spree, returning with a car load of smoked salmon, caviar, bottles of champagne, chocolates and presents for Timothy. But the local bills were never paid and mounted up until the butcher, baker and milkman all stopped coming. Word got round and our custom was not welcomed in any of the nearby shops. We often ran out of basic foods. Meanwhile, the investigation into Wheelan's death continued and Buddy Matter had to attend several courts in the nearby town of Horgen.

In June Rolf was sent on assignment to Rijeka in what was then Yugoslavia. A large industrial seaport on the Adriatic, its main import was oil from Romania. So we set off on what came to be a terrible journey. We travelled through the mountains by car, crossing into Italy and heading south to Venice. The strain between Rolf and Buddy became increasingly unbearable for all, and especially Timothy. Nearing Mestre, Buddy complained of a severe migraine and said she didn't wish to continue the journey. Thereupon Rolf drew up at the railway station where Buddy got out with her luggage. As she did so, Rolf leaned out of the window and casually told her that the case to be brought against her would be on a count of murder. With these words, he drove slowly round a corner out of sight. There we three sat in utter silence for about an hour. Rolf then returned to the station, collected Buddy, still awaiting a train, and returned to the car. We all continued to Venice.

Eventually we crossed the border at Trieste and drove on to the exclusive seaside resort of Opatija on the Dalmation coast. Rooms were reserved for us at the Dverner Hotel (a one-time summer residence of the Emperor Franz Joseph of Austria). I do not wish to linger too long on this bizarre and tragic six-week period. Suffice to say that, within a few days, Rolf picked up a girlfriend. One evening after entertaining guests in the absence of Rolf, Buddy went up to their bedroom and found her drunken husband on the bed. In the ensuing fight to obtain the car keys, she was badly knocked about, resulting in the near loss of one eye. I carried her to my room and kept her and Timothy there for the rest of the night. Rolf left for Switzerland the next day.

Having stayed beyond the time for which we had reserved, we were forced to leave our rooms and go into the hotel annexe, sharing one room. With her husband gone Buddy settled down to courting as much adulation and admiration as possible and fell in with a young Yugoslav doctor. Within the week he was often in our room, checking her health. We ran out of money and returned to Italy for further funds, to be obtained through Buddy's bank account. Bringing undeclared money into Yugoslavia was strictly forbidden, so I smuggled a wad inside a sanitary towel.

Buddy was mentally a very sick woman and dangerously unpredictable. When I told her I was leaving she gave me just enough money for the rail fare back to Zurich, and I last saw her lying on a sunbed, glass of wine in hand. Back in Au, I packed up my belongings and took train across the Channel to England. I never heard of them again.

* * * * *

Other tutoring jobs took me twice to Germany, and then I decided to try teaching again in a school. I went up to Scotland to look at a place near Montrose. The school was on high ground overlooking the sea and peacocks strutted about the lawns. It was rather remote, and the headmaster could only offer me a very small bedroom, more like a box room, and not even a bathroom to myself. It was definitely not my cup of tea. I looked at another non-starter before going a little south to my Crawford cousins near St Andrews. The three children had been laid low with hepatitis and their mother, Philippa, was really poorly. So began an extended and very happy few months. After the young had returned to school, Phil took a much needed convalescence with friends in Malta and I kept house, cooked and generally looked after Cousin Henry. The Crawfords were shortly due to move into the fine Adam house on the Naughton estate, where Henry was running the 3,000 acres.

Autumn 1961 and I was once again job hunting. Colin and I went up to London for a few days to see friends, and while there I dropped in on a number of scholastic agencies, among them one in Sloane Street which I liked. Miss Grey, a senior member of the agency, told me I had just missed a good position with the then British Ambassador in Jordan. I remember standing on the pavement pondering which agency to tackle next and then crossing over to Cadogan Square, a stone's throw away. There I was inundated with sheet after sheet of potentially winning positions in complete disregard for my specific requests. Anyway, an hour or so later I found myself at the Foreign Office being grilled by Jane Burton, Head of the Middle East Desk. She passed me on to a colleague for further questioning and all this with a view to taking up a position as governess to ten-year old Princess Basma bint Talal, the sister of His Majesty King Hussein of Jordan. I went home that evening quite exhausted. A couple of weeks later I was asked to attend Her Majesty Queen Zein at Claridge's for an interview.

I stayed with a friend who persuaded me to drink a gin and tonic at lunch to boost my morale for the afternoon's appointment. This was all very well, but I then had to use a mouthwash and clean my teeth several times to expunge all reek of alcohol. The queen spoke only in French which was a bit hard, but very soon asked me to come out to Jordan before the end of the year. Colin had only recently returned from three years' service in Malaysia and I much wanted to spend Christmas with him and my parents. So it was agreed that I should fly out to Amman in January, which I duly did.

The Hashemite royal family originated from that part of Arabia known as the Hejaz. Princess Basma's great grandfather, Sharif Hussein of Mecca, had been hereditary Guardian of the Holy Places of Islam, and a leading protagonist in the fight for Arab freedom from the Ottomans. Her grandfather, Emir and later King Abdullah I of Jordan, made Amman his capital. His assassination inside the Al Aqsa Mosque in Jerusalem in 1952 brought not only great shock, but the potential for instability to such a young country. His grandson Hussein, standing beside him, was miraculously saved from death when another bullet ricocheted off a medal on his uniform. Abdullah's son Talal acceded to the throne, but ill-health caused him to abdicate very soon in favour of the eighteen-year-old Hussein.

I arrived in Amman late at night and was met by two other members of staff, Frieda Muller, the Dutch dame d'accompagnie to the queen, and Norah Smith, an English nanny looking after six-year-old Princess Alia, daughter of the king and his first wife, Queen Dina. It wasn't until the next morning that Basma and I were 'formally' introduced. I had a room to myself, but spent much time with Basma. Here, I introduced her to Scottish dancing, playing the records I had brought from England and teaching her some of the steps. This was not very easy on a thickly carpeted floor and we had many laughs.

So I came to know a family of three brothers and their young sister. The king had recently married a second time and his English wife, Princess Muna, was expecting a child. The second brother, Mohammad, who suffered from asthma, spent time between Switzerland and Jordan. Hassan, at thirteen, was about to go to Harrow and also lived with us at Zahran Palace.

Basma was attending the excellent Church Missionary Society Ahliyyah School for Girls and I learnt that Queen Zein intended to send her daughter to boarding school in England fairly soon. I felt it was important for Basma to have extra coaching and undertook to give her lessons at home. This proved to be a difficult hurdle for Queen Zein, since it meant taking Basma out of school except for her Arabic lessons. Fortunately, I was supported by the strong minded headmistress, Mrs Bulos, and eventually we won through. So Basma had two consecutive Arabic lessons first thing, then I collected her for the rest of the morning's study at Zahran. It was hard work for us both, but Basma proved to be a very fine student and most conscientious. I was strict and demanded high standards, but hope I was fair, and I always believed in giving as much praise and encouragement as possible.

For recreation there was riding and during the winter months, when the horses went down to stables in the Jordan Valley, it was so pleasant to hack alongside banana plantations or canter across expanses of flat untilled fields. Birthday parties were rather a nightmare. Youngsters did not mingle together easily, especially if the sexes were mixed. I would draw up a list for the queen's approval, and in due course invitations were extended to those she considered 'suitable'. The boys came in suits and girls in very fancy party dresses, the more expensive the better. After all, it was a chance to show off how much money parents spent on these outward trappings. To break the ice and encourage the young guests to mingle, I pinned the name of a famous person on the back of each child. They had to ask one another questions to discover the name on their back. Party games consisted of musical chairs, treasure hunt, statues, pass the parcel and so forth. All pretty ordinary, you might think, but remember this took place within the queen's huge salon where boisterous behaviour was not encouraged.

Tea was at last announced and we all trooped across the passage to the dining room. The table groaned with plates of tiny sandwiches, sausage rolls, bureks, spiced biscuits and a birthday cake; it was de rigeur to fill every available space with a dish. Since there was no outside entertainment, the greatest fun came from the opening of presents. Big is beautiful: many a gift was too large for the child to carry and was brought in by the chauffeur. As the paper was ripped off and flung down, I frantically tried to match present with donor and compile a thank you list.

Life for my charge was restricted. There was only one shop we were allowed to visit called Toyland, owned by an Armenian. Outings consisted of going for a drive or, quite frequently, stopping by some flat ground to let Basma kick a ball about with myself, her guard and driver before turning round and heading for home. Picnics were unknown and her friends carefully screened by the queen. Three girls were found to be acceptable and were permitted to come over and play occasionally. I tried teaching them tennis without any success.

In May 1962 Queen Zein left for her usual summer visit to Europe. A few days later, Basma complained of a severe pain on her right side. The doctor was called and diagnosed appendicitis. He recommended an immediate operation. So to the Palestine Hospital we went, poor Basma very scared. The king was notified and duly arrived at the hospital just as his sister was being wheeled to the theatre. I walked alongside holding her hand and then came back to wait. Immediately, His Majesty told me to return to the theatre and attend the operation. Bereft of words, I did just that and after being gowned and masked, I stood beside Dr Sami Khoury, founder and chief surgeon of the hospital, as he chattily explained his procedures. There was no time to be apprehensive, or feel queasy at the sight of blood; I might have been attending a classroom lecture. All went well and after our return to Zahran Palace His Majesty presented me with a beautiful gold Omega watch. (Alas, many years later it was stolen from my house.)

Being a keen rider, I soon learnt about the royal stables. Eventually I persuaded the queen to allow Basma to have riding lessons and in time we enjoyed some pleasant hours on horseback. I gradually widened Basma's horizons, not only by taking her out more – and finally to Petra – but by reading to her and telling her stories of my own childhood in India.

So the months went by. Basma grew in stature and we had a lot of fun, too. Just as well, since there was little to no social life for me. Unless you had contacts outside, no one knew of your existence. Of course visitors were not allowed and free time was at a premium. I had insisted on having a contract, which clearly stated my job description, salary, free time and paid annual holiday. The result was that, unlike my colleagues at the palace, I did get one day off a week and a fortnight's leave.

In November 1962, we travelled with Queen Zein to London. The queen was anxious to see some places of further education for her daughter as well as to have a shopping spree before Christmas. I had already acquired a number of prospectuses from different schools for her perusal, and she appeared especially interested in Benenden in Kent.

So we drove down to meet the noted and somewhat formidable (aren't they all?) headmistress of the school, Miss Betty Clarke. The queen always spoke to us in French, but could converse in English. However, on this occasion she preferred not to do so, and I was left to translate. I knew that in certain subjects, particularly the sciences, Basma was not quite up to standard, so I plugged her considerable ability at languages. Miss Clarke agreed to accept Basma for the autumn term of 1963.

I was now official guardian to Basma during term time, and returned to my family in Wiltshire. Little did I know what was in store!

8

John O'Neill had been a young subaltern in my father's regiment. Coming down from Oxford just prior to the war, he had decided on a military career with the Indian Army. It was obligatory to be fluent in Urdu and, in order to gain experience of regimental life and have sufficient time for language study, he spent a year seconded to a British regiment serving in India.

Once established with the XV Punjab Regiment, John loved the camaraderie and challenges of regimental life. He was an exceptional shot and enjoyed sports. This was most important, as a considerable part of the junior officers' time was bound up with their men. Apart from drill, parades and military exercises, sport was a means of keeping fit and induced a competitive spirit, where each platoon took pride in coming first.

John was posted to Burma during the war and served there with the XIX Dagger Division throughout most of the campaign. It was a bloody and relentless time of gains and losses, terrible jungle terrain and frequent sickness. The Japanese guerrilla tactics gave no room for let up, and exhaustion was always at each man's shoulder.

During one particularly bold attack, several of John's fellow officers were killed and his Commanding Officer severely wounded. John immediately took command, allowing no man time to waver. With drive and initiative he regrouped his troops and made a swift and decisive counter attack, holding the Japanese off until reinforcements arrived. For his cool headed action, courage and inspired leadership, John was awarded the DSO (Distinguished Service Order).

Of course, I only learnt of all these events much later. By the end of the war, John was not only exhausted but suffering from severe ulcerative colitis, and spent some time at a convalescent home in Yorkshire. There he met Barbara who was working as a VAD (Voluntary Aid Detachment). These women provided basic nursing services in the field, but mainly in hospitals. John and Barbara became engaged and were married at Chester Cathedral in 1946. Although John's career as an Indian Army officer ended with Partition in 1947, he and Barbara were in Quetta while John studied at the Staff College, after which he joined the British Army. They returned to England and were posted to Wales. Patrick was born in 1948 and their second son Kim in 1950.

Having been promoted to Lieutenant Colonel, John was posted to Washington DC as a member of the British team and part of the NATO Standing Group at the Pentagon. It was after his return from the States and following a routine medical check that he was found to have chronic myoloid leukaemia. This meant no possible foreign postings and he was appointed as G2 at Nottingham. Very tragically, while John and Barbara were holidaying in Scotland in 1961, they were involved in a car accident in which Barbara died.

My parents had kept up with John and later, when he was posted to Southern Command as G1 to General Mike Carver, they saw him again. In December 1962 I was briefly in England with Queen Zein and Basma on a Christmas shopping spree and had obtained her permission to spend two nights with my parents. John was invited to lunch and we met there for the first time.

I remember entering the drawing room to join the trio and being struck by John's considerable height: 6 feet 4 inches! He was slim, well dressed in cavalry twill trousers and blazer, and he greeted me with much charm and warmth. It was a pleasant meeting, and after lunch we stood chatting at the edge of the river which ran through the garden. I returned to Jordan and did not get back to England until the following September, on my appointment as guardian to Princess Basma throughout the period she would be attending school at Benenden.

Completing his time with General Carver at Wilton, John was promoted, and appointed as Colonel MO4 at the Ministry of Defence in London. His area covered Africa (less West Africa), Aden, Radfan, the Persian Gulf and Jordan.

On my return to England, I was surprised and amazed to find John at the airport, but it was very nice to see him and I was really touched

The *Daily Telegraph* picture of King Hussein's visit to Benenden School
when leaving his sister there, September 1963

at his thought. A week later Basma flew into Heathrow in the company of His Majesty and his younger brother Crown Prince Hassan. I joined them a day or so later when we all travelled by car, HM at the wheel, to Benenden School in Kent. There we were met by Miss Kirwan, Basma's house-mistress, and another girl, Veronica Bowring, who had been appointed as 'guardian' to Basma during her first days at school to help her become orientated into a very new situation. I was dressed in a tweed suit with hat and gloves, walking a few steps behind the king, and I was entertained the next day to see that the front page of The Daily Telegraph was adorned with a large black and white picture of the royal party, including myself. The best part, though, was the caption which read, 'King of Jordan's sister to join Princess Anne at

Benenden School. From left to right: Queen Zein (me), Princess Basma ... Miss Kirwan (house mistress) and King Hussein, seen walking in the grounds of Benenden School after leaving his sister.' It's not every day that one is mistaken for royalty!

I expected to spend a little time at home, looking around for some useful occupation, but always bearing in mind that I might be summoned to a school function, to take Basma out, or to travel to London with her for a dental visit.

John had a very nice army quarter in Bulford village, about thirty minutes' drive from our house, and I found myself going over there increasingly frequently when John would ring me for some horticultural advice while working in the garden during his weekends. We became very easy and happy together and one October afternoon, after climbing a hill behind the village, we sat on the grass to watch the sun go down and John began to tell me of his leukaemia. He also told me of his love for me and asked me to marry him. I simply turned to him and said, 'Yes,' with not one moment's hesitation. I asked that we keep the news to ourselves for a few days, just to savour the happiness and joy of it all. Then John came over to my place and in time honoured fashion, asked my father for my hand.

Things moved pretty fast after that. Only John's brother knew of his illness, not even his boys, and that was how he wanted it. But there was nothing to wait for, and John was due to move yet again almost immediately after Christmas and wished to settle into his new quarter with a wife.

On 25th January 1964 at the lovely old church of St Andrew, Nunton, near Salisbury, John and I were wed. It was a most joyous occasion only blotted, literally, by fog, yes, dense fog, which made it impossible to see from the lych gate to the church door, or for the photographer to take a clear picture of us leaving the church!

We left that behind and headed for Heathrow and a wonderfully happy two weeks in Majorca. Returning to Bulford and immediately packing up to move to an army quarter at West Byfleet was not so jolly

– for me, anyway. Once back, John was immersed in work and I had to knuckle down to getting things ready for the move.

Apart from unpacking at the other end and creating as much of a home atmosphere as I could in an uninspiring army house, I was preparing myself for a closer situation with my two stepsons. Except for being at their father's wedding, I had hardly met them during that autumn term. Now John and I were together, there would be school visits, exeats, and the first family holiday as 'mum'. This was somewhat daunting, I recall only too well.

Patrick was fifteen and at Malvern, while Kim at thirteen would shortly join him. They were very different from one another. Pat had high expectations from life and from those around him who could help him onto the ladder of success. To make money was his ambition and he had a good brain to put to it. I am sure that I didn't come anywhere near his expectations, but we managed fairly well. I tried to remember the tragedy of Barbara's sudden death and the shock and terrible loss it must have been. With Kim, our relationship was altogether different. He had much of John's easy, companionable personality and enjoyed being around the house; even as a youngster, he liked to take a hand at baking. He was both deft and adept with his hands, often helping John with wiring in the house or doing a bit of carpentry.

I had learnt how to cook as I grew up at home and my mother was a very good teacher, but for so many years I had lived and worked abroad where cooking was not requisite to my job as a tutor. Now I had to produce full-blown meals for three hungry males. I have never been very good with meat. Knowing about joints was almost double Dutch to me, and even more worrying was the right length of time to cook it. But I soldiered on and tried to be a modern mother and understand the jargon and habits of the day. I really knew so little of British living habits, so to speak, and television was an eye opener. My family were absolute devotees, but all through our years together, and since, I never got the bug to watch it for any length of time.

I continued to be Basma's guardian in England and, of course, John joined me following our marriage. Basma was very fond of him and called him 'Twinkle'. At the beginning of each term John and I met her at Heathrow, generally in the Alcock and Brown Suite, often bumping into other members of the Hashemite royals. She would spend a night or two with us before I took her back to Benenden by train. So from Zahran Palace in Amman, she slept in an army quarter and shared in all the activities of a family at home – helping around the house, going for walks and sometimes doing a little shopping. When Basma's exeats didn't coincide with the boys', we liked to show her something of England and Scotland. We had some wonderful holidays: Guernsey and a boat trip to Sark; the Isle of Wight and a visit to Osborne House, the one time home of Queen Victoria; the New Forest; and a very special stay in Scotland with my Crawford cousins in their beautiful Adams house. There, Basma slept in a period room furnished entirely by the famed cabinet maker, Thomas Sheraton, from the tester bed down to the daintiest matchbox.

John's job was extremely interesting, but demanding. Throughout the early sixties many African countries were gaining their independence, and it was part of John's remit to prepare the ground for and travel with the Foreign Secretary on his official visits to these new states. He flew several times with Duncan Sandys and regaled me about some of the happenings. Sandys suffered constant pain from a war wound, and not surprisingly this affected his behaviour, particularly on long haul flights. He became quite irascible and one of his relaxations was to play Scrabble. Naturally John was drawn into the fray, but there were lighter moments, like a flight to the Victoria Falls. John sent me a concertina card depicting the magnificence and immensity of the falls. Was I envious! Other times he would arrive home, laden with avocados or pineapple.

While still at the Ministry of Defence, in 1966 John received a letter informing him that he was to be awarded a CBE. I was so excited but the news had to be kept quiet until it was publicly announced in the paper.

In due course John was posted to Old Sarum and, since there was no quarter suitable to his rank, we joyfully hired a house on the edge of the New Forest. It was a very happy time, living in a hamlet and becoming part of a rural community with acres of lovely heathland on which to walk and exercise our dog, Buck. It was from here that Patrick, Kim and I travelled with John to London and Buckingham Palace to see him receive his CBE from Her Majesty the Queen. A truly proud moment and a decoration so richly deserved, I know.

John shortly after receiving his CBE in 1966

Meanwhile, Basma continued to come and go between the UK and Jordan, and always stayed with us for a few days. Queen Zein invited me to Amman in 1967. It was strange to be back in my old room at Zahran, yet a visitor. Frieda Muller was in charge of our excursions, and together with Basma, joined by her three friends, we travelled by car to Aqaba for a short stay. It is interesting to recall what the desert highway was like in those days. It was just two way and, after dropping down from Ma'an, the steep sharp bends were extremely hazardous, particularly for heavy vehicles. Once down in the area of Wadi Rum the road ran its own course and we were met with shallow dips every 500 yards. This made for very tiring and uncomfortable driving. Nevertheless, we all thoroughly enjoyed the few days swimming and shopping in Aqaba's varied and oriental bazaar.

Meanwhile, my family at home grumbled at my absence, and that was the only time I was parted from them. We moved twice in the New Forest before John was posted in March 1969 to Western Command at Chester as the Colonel AQ. He phoned me the news, and to this day I remember the chill and darkness that came over me. He and Barbara had been married in Chester Cathedral and it seemed to me with a terrible force that his married life had begun there and would end there. I dreaded packing up and going, but that was it, and I kept all my misgivings to myself. We had a pleasant Victorian house directly opposite the headquarters, so John had no distance to walk. For this I was immensely thankful. At the beginning of 1969, while we were still living in our own house at East Knoyle in Wiltshire, he went down with pneumonia – in itself not too serious with excellent and fast-acting drugs, but for a man with leukaemia, a different story. The pneumonia was cured, but at considerable cost to John's stamina. From then on, it was a struggle with misbalance of his blood cells and platelets and increasing debility and tiredness.

In the summer of 1969, John received an official letter from the Jordanian Ambassador in London. In it he informed us that His Majesty King Hussein had graciously bestowed on John the Order of Istiklal, and on me, the Order of the Star of Jordan. This was not only a complete surprise but a great honour for us both. The citation read, 'For services to the Hashemite Royal Family.'

In due course, John and I journeyed to London and received our decorations from the hands of the Ambassador. John's is on a maroon ribbon and mine on a green one. There was just the one occasion to wear them: a grand reception held at Lancaster House for all the diplomatic heads. The evening was part of the celebrations to mark the Investiture of the Prince of Wales at Caernarfon Castle on 1 July 1969. John had been responsible for the final security details of the ceremony. My dress of emerald coloured silk beautifully set off my amethyst necklace and earrings.

Now in Chester, I was busy with a large house and entertaining, but was never really happy there and suffered a lot of pain in my left arm, to such an extent that I could barely use it. Eventually I went to see a specialist in London who told me it was mainly due to living so close to the river and its consequent dampness. Sure enough, after I moved it soon disappeared.

Basma had left Benenden in the summer of 1968, having attained excellent A-levels in French and Spanish, and the boys were preparing for the world. Patrick came down from Oxford with a law degree and Kim was in his second year at Dartmouth.

In September John and I drove north to Scotland where John had been invited for some stag shooting, and before that we were going to relax with army friends on Mull. It soon became apparent that John's health was not good and we sadly gave up the rest of the holiday and drove to my parents' home near Drumnadrochit. From there I took John to the Inverness Infirmary where he received – for the first time ever – a blood transfusion. A few days later we made the long journey down to Chester and John continued straight on to London and into St Bartholomew's hospital. He was immediately seen by his haematologist, Sir Ronald BodleyScott.

There was a marked deterioration in his health and, although I never gave up hope that rest and medication would give an improved balance to the disease, as the days and weeks passed I had to face some terrible facts. One evening after saying goodnight to John and leaving the ward, I was accosted by the senior registrar who asked me into his office. There, in very blunt terms he told me that John had little time to live. He wished me good evening and left. I can never erase that time from memory. I had just bought an attractive green outfit and worn it for the first time specially to look good for my visit. I left the hospital and the rain was falling gently from a cloudy night sky. Walking towards St. Paul's Cathedral to catch a bus, I was absolutely lost. I struggled in an agony of mind and tears just poured down. I knew I must lift my head to gain any control and courage and, as I did so, I said to myself words from Psalm 21 which have always been a solace and comfort to me: 'I will lift up mine eyes unto the hills from whence cometh my help…'. I never wore that outfit again and soon gave it away.

John came home once for a weekend. I pretended to myself that he was hopefully in remission, but seeing him sitting at his desk and going through all private papers and will, I knew I was only kidding myself. He was so thin and barely ate. At night he would wake up drenched in sweat and I would dry and change him several times. It was terribly frightening for me, but I managed to remain as calm and normal as possible. I realized how important it was for him to feel my presence without panic.

After his return to St. Bartholomew's, I spoke to Sir Ronald and arranged for John to be moved to the King Edward VII Hospital for Officers in Beaumont Street. He now had a private room and I was free to come at any time. It was there that Princess Basma came to visit him.

Sir Ronald did everything he possibly could, including trying an entirely new drug not yet on the market. By the beginning of December I had to make some decisions. The fact that John had never told his parents or his sons about his illness made it very difficult to broach the subject with him. With Patrick working in Chester and Kim at sea in the Far East, they had to be informed. John didn't want to see anyone but me, although my brother-in-law, Michael, knew the facts. After consultation with Sir Ronald, Michael stood by to bring my mother-in-law up from Cornwall while I received much assistance in flying Kim back from Hong Kong and, of course, Patrick came down from Chester. We gathered at the hospital, though John did not know this and only wanted me. Later, Michael took the group out for a meal and I sat with John that evening of 11th December 1969. No one knew how long he had, a day or two, perhaps more. Sometime around seven o'clock, as I sat close to him, I sensed a stillness and knew instinctively that my beloved husband had left me. I was all alone and cried out, not in shock, but as if my soul had left my body. Matron took care of me, and I waited for the family with the news I would have to give them. So much grief for each of us, and for my mother-in-law a terrible blow. I took her hand and at her wish left her to have a little time alone with John. For the boys it was too much of an ordeal. It was getting very late and arrangements had to be made for Patrick and Kim to stay with relatives. So we were all scattered. My father came to take me to my lodgings and I climbed the stairs to my small bedroom. I was outside myself and undressed without thinking. No feeling, just numb. I tried to say my prayers, but felt nothing. I only knew that there was another day awaiting me with dreadful burdens.

So the coming days demanded all the tasks associated with death: an announcement in the paper, funeral arrangements and deciding where I wanted John to be buried. While living in the New Forest, John and I had attended the little church at Hyde which serves several small villages. Here in the peaceful churchyard with such happy memories, I wanted John to rest. His general at that time had been Billy Barton, who kindly obtained the necessary permission. Dear Colin was a tower of strength and arranged for a piper to play the Last Post. So many kind people attended the service to share my grief. Michael brought my mother-in-law from Cornwall, but my father-in-law refused to come, on the grounds of the inconvenience with his prostate. He had refused to marry us and never visited John while he was in hospital. Come to think of it, he had even declined ever to come and stay. Although a priest for many years, he was a strange, rather sad man. He carried a grudge against life that seemed to colour so many of his actions. I think he was unhappy too but, never sharing himself with his wife or sons, he must have been truly lonely.

Several years after John's death, while I was visiting my parents-in-law, Papa suddenly began a tirade on the lack of care and proper treatment John had received. I was shocked at this outburst and terribly hurt and upset. It felt like a body blow and I told him to stop talking about it immediately. For one who hadn't been near his son once during his time of suffering, he had no right to open his mouth. It's strange how these brief moments linger so long and sharply in the mind. I feel the pain to this day.

Christmas was almost on us, and the boys and I were invited to stay with dear friends who lived near Cheltenham. How wonderfully sensitive and understanding they were. I slept in Ken and Mary Mead's charming cottage and Patrick and Kim were nearby with Mary's brother, who farmed and had sons of his own. Mary was a wonderful person, immensely kind and thoughtful, wise and so easy to talk to. She and Ken had known John long before I met him, but from the time of our engagement the Meads took me to their hearts, and their affection was immediately reciprocated. I think it was the start of a healing and strengthening time for me, although that would be a long road.

After Christmas Kim had to return to his ship and I to our quarter in Chester. Patrick was preparing for his flight out to Canada to take up a job with a mining company in the northwest. In January 1970 I saw him off from Manchester Airport, and then I was really alone. Of course I had to vacate the army quarter and move everything back to our own house near Warminster, which was let. The couple who had rented it were extremely understanding and agreed to leave early. So I began the mammoth task of sorting all our possessions. I was very blessed in having a wonderful batwoman, Joan, who worked tirelessly, doing much of the cleaning as I prepared for the packers. We got on so well and I learnt much about her family and some of the hardships she faced. That was a good thing as it gave me thought for someone else and kept the bouts of loneliness and self-pity at bay.

For the final days I stayed overnight with two couples. They were so good to me, never intruding, but seeing to my every comfort and offering a wonderful meal with them at night. The normality of their behaviour was the greatest help; I cannot stress enough how beneficial this can be for anyone suffering deep loss. Interesting conversation, laughter, just warm friendliness is a balm to the ultra sensitivity of aching grief.

Eventually the time came for my departure from Chester. It had snowed the day before and, coward that I was, I hoped that would give me safe haven and further respite for a few more days. But the snow went and the sun shone and I had to step out into the real world and face life alone. I had a Mini Minor station wagon and, together with my suitcases, there was Buck, our Labrador-cross sheepdog. To calm my nerves I talked incessantly to Buck or myself, as we drove along unfamiliar roads and on frighteningly fast motorways. Late that afternoon I made it to East Knoyle and our house. Here I faced another terrible hurdle: to walk up the path, open the front door to a house empty of furniture, empty of John.

Dear village friends, Ronnie and Mary Macdonald, kindly invited me to stay during the unpacking. Finally one evening there was another more permanent challenge, to drive back to the house, open the door, walk in and lock it behind me. I didn't know how I was going to bear being in the empty bed, so I chose to sleep on John's 'side' and felt comforted. I have done that ever since.

* * * * *

I had little news from Patrick after his departure for northern Canada. The job he had been promised never materialized, and I give him full credit for staying on in Canada and moving to Vancouver where he was offered work with an import–export firm. It was hard and very challenging since many young men were out of work at that time and looking for a foothold with a decent company. Patrick obviously made an impression, for some time later he was recommended by his employers to move to a similar but more interesting position in Japan. There he settled in well, met Reiko, and they were married at St. Albans church in Tokyo. Two daughters, Emiko and Mariko, were born to them after their return to the UK. Pat is a workaholic. After several years commuting to London from their home in Surrey, he is now working in Singapore.

My younger stepson, Kim, was still at Dartmouth Naval College and would be passing out that summer. In the meanwhile I continued to live in East Knoyle and busied myself with village life, but it was not my choice to remain there alone for the foreseeable future and I felt, too, that I had more to give than 'good works' and selling produce at Women's Institutes.

I moved to London and stayed as a paying guest of an old friend of my parents. There were plenty of temporary jobs to be had, especially if one knew London well. So I found myself some good, some bad and some downright atrocious employment. Most of my employers were wealthy Americans or Greeks coming to London for medical treatment or business, and for the ladies, of course, 'the shopping'. They took suites at either Claridge's, Grosvenor House or the Dorchester, and there I met their offspring. What a loutish lot most of them were – frightfully spoilt, bad mannered, rude and totally uninterested in any of the many sights and exhibitions I took them to. I remember two particular Greek teenagers coming into the dining room at Claridge's and as we passed the trolley filled with hors d'oeuvres, the elder girl stretched out her hand and took some prawns, stuffing them into her mouth as the waiter looked on aghast. You can imagine what I thought. Fortunately these periods of employment were brief, usually a week at most, but the mother of this particular family took a shine to me and, on the last day when her husband was winding up some lucrative shipping deal, she asked me in all seriousness if I would join them and travel back to Greece. She was looking for a lady's maid and thought I would fit the bill very nicely. I graciously declined.

Other families would arrive in London, rent an apartment and then leave me to feed, care for and entertain their young whilst they were out all day. Thank goodness I never slept on the premises, and usually returned to my friend's house, quite drained.

1. The order of Al-Kawkab Al-Urduni (Star of Jordan), bestowed by His Majesty King Hussein on Ann O'Neill, July 1969

2. Lake Tiberias, a view from Umm Qais, Jordan

3. Last of the harvest, Tel el-Rumman, Jordan

4. Colin and Anne's wedding at St. John's Church, Edinburgh, 14th August 1972

5. Springtime in my garden, Umm Uthaina, Amman

6. Thousands of trees are bound with rope as winter protection, a common sight when travelling along the roads. South Korea 1986

7. By early May, after the bitter winter, street vendors of Seoul are out with their brilliant displays of bedding plants.

8. Dendarah. The Roman Sanctuary with five columns, taken from the roof of the Temple, Egypt 1987

9. The Colossi of Memnon standing alone across the River Nile from Luxor

10. A gift from Keiko, my five year old Japanese student

11. Vera and Tania from Russia, two of my favourite students

12. Little Keiko, who used to say "I love learning!"

13. Corinthian columns at Salamis,
Cyprus 1991

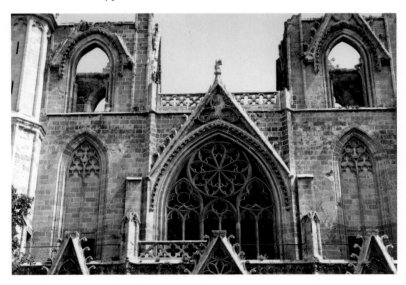

14. Ruins of St. Nicholas Cathedral at Famagusta. It was converted to a mosque
in 1571, following Turkish bombardment. Note part of a minaret on the left.

15. Ready with my craft display at the German Ladies' Bazaar in Amman, Christmas 1996

16. Steel drums to be driven 80 metres into the sand then filled with concrete, forming part of the construction of the Bangabundhu Bridge, Bangladesh 1997

9

Shortly after that, I left London and settled back into my house in East Knoyle with some plans to be made, bearing in mind that while Kim was still at Dartmouth, this would be his home. I attended his passing out summer ball, but although we were a group of friends, it was sad and lonely for me with no partner and standing alone a good deal of the evening.

Almost immediately, Kim began a year's course at Culdrose, training as a helicopter observer. He did extremely well, and at the end of the year was awarded the much prized Daedalus Cup for the best student. How proud John would have been.

The following year, the wedding of Colin and Anne took place at St. John's Church in Edinburgh on 14th August 1971. Colin wore the full dress uniform of his regiment, the Royal Highland Fusiliers, and looked so handsome in his Mackenzie tartan trews. Pipe Major D. W. Aitken BEM of the regimental band wrote, 'Major Colin Mackenzie's Wedding March' for the occasion. We were all very touched by the attendance of Clevie and Mary Jane Cleveland, a delightful American couple whom my father had escorted through England several times as a guide.

Thinking about it, I knew that odd jobs in London were not my cup of tea and started to look around for a private teaching position, preferably abroad. Once again I toured the employment agencies and, in due course, I was offered and accepted the position of governess to a granddaughter of the Shah of Iran. That was in the autumn. Upon going to the Iranian Embassy to collect my visa and air ticket to Tehran, however, I was told that the Shah had changed his mind and intended instead to send the sixteen-year-old girl to the American School. I remember feeling very miffed and, while I was preparing to leave, an official asked me to stay and meet someone who might well be interested to interview me.

Shortly after, a small, expensively dressed and somewhat perfumed man entered the room and I was introduced to HE Mr Hushang Ansary, the Iranian Minister of Economy. We talked, or, rather, he talked and told me that he and his wife were looking for a governess for their two young children. He could immediately arrange my documents and fly me out within the next week at the latest.

Now, I am someone who very much trusts my instincts and I must say that, except for a few occasions, I have not been misled. I made a mistake this time, though. I had not taken to Hushang, nor did I like the fact that he wore dark glasses throughout the interview. But because I had set my heart on going to live in Iran, I brushed aside any misgivings and agreed to his terms.

So November 1971 found me winging my way to Tehran, arriving there on a cold, pouring night. Of course I didn't see the children until the next morning. At five and six and a half, Nader and Nadereh were pretty spoilt and ill-disciplined. Their mother, Mariam, was Hushang Ansary's second wife. Mariam's father had been ambassador at the Court of St James and her mother equally patrician. So Hushang, a man of ability but humble background, successfully climbed the ladder of ambition. He had the brains; she had background and money.

Mariam was some years younger than her husband and immensely vain. She generally arose between ten and eleven o'clock, had a light breakfast in her room and then dressed to go out for coffee with friends, shopping for the latest modes. At least twice a week the driver took her down to the Hilton for a coiffure and manicure.

I quickly settled the children into a routine, but was continuously hampered by their mother, who, when they were dressed, would come in and decide she didn't like the clothes they were wearing and that they didn't match one another. I took them to school each morning, and after lunch at home we had lessons together.

Lunch was always a nightmare. We three ate alone and, whatever we had, they generally didn't want it. It was obvious that they did as they liked at the table, throwing food at each other, getting up and down at will, shouting at the cook for something else. So it was a constant exhausting battle at each meal. Mariam came in from time to time and, seeing small helpings being pushed around the plates, she invariably complained that they didn't have enough to eat, piled on the rice – then left. Lunch could take up to an hour of stress and effort to get food down them. In fact, when they continually refused it, I told them to leave the table since they were obviously not hungry. You can imagine that did not go down well with mama, but by evening their appetite had suddenly returned and they were glad to eat what had been spurned earlier.

It was a very lonely job. Most evenings the Ansarys were out and I wasn't allowed to invite friends in. It didn't take me long to dislike the atmosphere in which I lived and the type of people I was obliged to meet when taking the children to 'weekend' lunches with their parents. A typical Thursday or Friday would mean dressing Nader and Nadereh in their finery, myself included, and tag along to our host's mansion for a gossipy morning among the ladies and bridge or generally Black Jack and whisky in another room for the men. I was completely ignored after the initial courtesies and had to amuse two very bored kids for several hours before lunch was announced. The vast dining room was hung with cut-glass chandeliers, a table displaying beautiful silverware, and waiters lined up to pull out the chairs and dispense their service.

The children and I were fortunately spared this and, after we three had finished our meal, I could take them out onto the verandah for a little fresh air. It was here that I was joined on several occasions by one of the male guests. After the usual opening gambit, this man seriously started to chat me up. Upon hearing my 'beautiful' English, it had occurred to him that what his wife and family and of course he himself needed, was tuition and conversation. He suggested a rendezvous where he and I might meet to discuss 'matters'. It took me no time to disabuse him of any latent ideas he might have had. What I found so offensive among this class of very rich and well educated Iranian men and women was their arrogance, and assumption that anything was available to be bought.

The weather throughout my three months in the Ansary household was grim. Snow fell heavily most days, and we always had chains on the car wheels when taking the children some miles down into Tehran for their schooling. It was virtually impossible to get out of the city and many times the airports were closed.

The Ansarys left for a two-week trip and I was on my own, except for the male cook and house boy. During that time Mariam's charming mother came over to see the grandchildren. What a complete contrast to her daughter! Well read, fluent in several languages, she was also a gifted conversationalist. It was such a pleasure to share some time with her.

After the parents' return, things became more strained and I found that when I returned late from my Sunday outing I was not allowed to use the front door, but had to go round the back and enter the house through the servants' bedroom. Picture me tiptoeing between the two beds.

One morning after dropping off the children, I entered the house and heard terrible shouting. At the top of the double flight of stairs, Mariam was standing in her negligée and screaming what was clearly abuse at the woman who cleaned all the marble floors. Her name was Shukofeh, which means blossom, and she and I had become friends in spite of the language barrier. She reminded me so much of the Palestinian women who do the same job in Jordan in hospitals and homes. What she had or had not done I didn't know, but something stuck in my mind and I was appalled at Mariam's behaviour.

Sunday was my one day off, when I attended the Anglican church. There I got to know Bill and Fay Pakenham Walsh. Bill was a senior military adviser at the newly formed military academy. They kindly invited me for Christmas Day and I had a most happy time with them and their two adopted children. In fact, if it hadn't been for Bill and Fay, I would not have lasted even three months in Iran with the Ansarys. Through them I discovered that there were many possibilities to teach in schools or privately and I was much in demand. When I was again present at one of Mariam's tirades, I decided to leave and shortly after gave in my notice. Unfortunately, being free of the Ansarys did not get me any further since I had been employed under their umbrella regarding residence in Iran and, once I left them, I was no longer legal.

So in February 1972 I packed my bags and flew to Jordan. And here I still am after more than forty years!

10

Queen Zein was kind enough to offer me a room in Zahran Palace while I looked around for work and a place of my own. This I duly found in April and moved into a totally bare villa with a small garden, no phone, no form of heating and no transport. Good friends rallied round and, with what money I had earned in Tehran, I bought, or rather, hired basic furniture and invested in some cheap moquette carpeting. Now that I had a roof over my head, all I needed was a job.

With my considerable teaching experience I had fondly and somewhat foolishly imagined I could find employment at the British Council in Amman or some other institution in need of an experienced English teacher. Without a degree or any educational diploma, however, they wouldn't look at me. So Queen Zein sent me to see the then Prime Minister Ahmed al-Lawzi, and to his office I sallied forth one morning. He regretted being unable to offer me a position, but referred me to the Director General of Jordan Television. I duly trotted off to JTV and met Mohammad Kamal. A tall, handsome, well-dressed man, Mr Kamal was also highly educated, having spent a considerable time working within the bureaux of the British Mandate in Jerusalem.

He at once sent me to the newly established educational department of JTV, and that same day after a voice test and talking to camera, I was taken on as the presenter of the English language programmes to be used in conjunction with the English curriculum in the state secondary schools. Television was a relatively new innovation in Jordan, and placing TV sets in the schools was a bold advance on education in the kingdom.

Together with a programme director supplied from the UK by the British Council, we worked together using themes of everyday life, each lesson closely co-ordinated with the teaching material in daily use. I would in no way describe myself as photogenic, so tried to make up for this lack by the liveliness of my delivery and trying to be as natural as possible. You must remember I had never been before cameras, let alone worked in a studio with glaring, dazzling lights constantly focused on me.

For some two years I worked in this field and, during that time, I became much more interested in the adjacent Radio Jordan. So, as well as my weekly educational output at JTV, I began to read the news in English on Radio Jordan and then to edit children's stories to be aired on Friday mornings. Together with a colleague, I recorded a series of live programmes on the flora of Jordan. That was difficult, since we literally had to ad lib and try not to cut across one another's words. Each week we had variously painted flowering plants displayed on the studio table, and referred to them as appropriate. They were certainly good 'gap' fillers!

In due course I left both Radio Jordan and the English teaching programme and moved to the Foreign Relations Department. The person responsible for this was Lina Gress. She had lost her father in the bombing of the King David Hotel, Jerusalem, in July 1946. She was a clever person with three languages at her fingertips, but of such a volatile temperament. Rarely still, she drove herself and others remorselessly, and appeared to have little liking or respect for other women, referring to them as, 'all fools!' I had been warned when she offered me the job that I wouldn't last six months. In fact, I managed three years before Lina stated one day that she was going to evict me. Luckily I had seen the writing on the wall for some time and had prepared the way for another job. So when she finally said that if I didn't leave immediately she would throw me out, I collected my things and left.

Over the years I had noted the casual and rather slack manner in which Mohammad Kamal's office was run, and decided he needed someone to take it in hand. I encouraged him in this notion and, when I left Lina, he was quite happy to give me a tiny office and tell me to get on with it. For seven years I was his 'PA' and because he disliked anything to do with administration he often left me to answer his letters (by telex) and if in writing, to sign on his behalf. Although I took the correspondence to the deputy director general, he usually told me it was not his responsibility and returned it to me with the words, 'I don't think I can undertake this. Please sign it yourself.' And I did, with a 'pp' first.

I was now well settled into an interesting and demanding job, but variety is the spice of life. In 1977 my friend Frieda Muller (dame d'accompagnie to Queen Zein) fell and broke her femur and was out of action for several months. As the time approached for the queen's yearly winter visit to Europe, it was decided that I should take Frieda's place for that month. Mr Kamal was approached and of course gave his consent.

Thus, out of the blue, I was whisked from my job as his PA to prepare myself for something entirely unexpected. As I would be constantly in attendance on Her Majesty, having some smart clothes was essential. I only possessed a few suitable dresses and one suit. Frieda kindly loaned me some pretty blouses and a skirt. With that and a nice overcoat, I was ready for the challenge.

We flew to Paris, staying at the renowned Hotel Meurice in the Rue de Rivoli. The queen's suite was that which the late Duke of Windsor had always used. The days in Paris were busy ones, with Christmas purchases to be made for all the family members and visits to the haute couture establishments for Her Majesty's wardrobe. Afternoon tea was always taken outside the hotel, a short distance along the arched street and into a patisserie offering the most delectable choice of gateaux. Since Her Majesty rarely took more than one piece, I also had to be abstemious.

During my brief leisure periods I quickly changed into some outdoor shoes and exiting from the hotel would cross the road and enter the Gardens of the Tuilleries. From there it was a short walk to the Louvre. I had barely two hours and made the most of every minute. Apart from the fabulous paintings, including the famed Mona Lisa, the very fabric of this place tells its own powerful story.

Two weeks later we boarded our train for the day long journey to Geneva. The landscape changed dramatically as we entered

Switzerland, the dense forest of fir trees on either side of the track already thickly covered in snow. From the station we drove to the Beau Rivage, situated on Lake Lucerne. The hotel had magnificent views across the water to the distant mountains. Now December, it was very cold, and I was grateful for the warmth of Her Majesty's apartments.

During the fortnight here, we took several pleasant drives along the lakeside, once to Montreux and on another occasion up into the mountains to enjoy the view and take tea at another venue again much favoured by the queen.

On our return to Jordan I resumed my work at JTV, reminiscing on some of the things I had learnt and on unusual aspects of a job I had never anticipated doing. It was a relief that I no longer had to converse in French all the time.

* * * * *

In the early spring of 1978 Frieda, Daphne Hobson (nanny to Princess Basma's children) and myself obtained permission from Queen Zein to make a trip to Damascus. With a four wheel drive and palace driver, we set off for a day's sightseeing and possible shopping in the souq. On arrival, we found the city packed with people and particularly dense along the route and entrance to the Friday Mosque in the old city. It was the Prophet Mohammad's birthday, and the motor cavalcade of Hafez al Assad, President of Syria, was just entering the street. Soldiers lining the route held the crowds back from crossing to the other side until the motorcade was well through the archway. They then stepped back and, as you may imagine, there was a massive surge of humanity as people pushed one way or the other across the street. We three, all unknowingly, had positioned ourselves on the street corner, ready to make our way up the same road into the city. The sheer press of humanity, however, had us floored in minutes. Frieda's hold on a lamp post was torn away and she fell down. Daphne told me she was literally tossed into the air and landed on the pavement some way away. I, too, was lying on my back; all I could do was to raise my legs and arms in an almost futile gesture against the trampling feet. I think we were incredibly fortunate that, being close to the edge of the road, the soldiers had heard cries and moved in swiftly among the crowd to rescue us. A kind shopkeeper took us in and sat us down on stools with cups of Turkish coffee. Daphne and I were pretty shaken and extensively bruised, but poor Frieda, still not too agile on her legs following the recovery from her broken femur, suffered a fractured collar bone and was in agony.

Here I must mention Mohammed, our driver. He was really magnificent and did all he could to shield Frieda. When we had gathered our strength, the next thing was to find a hospital and have Frieda's shoulder attended to. This was easier said than done. Being a public holiday, the outpatient departments were not functioning at all in the majority of hospitals and Mohammed made endless enquiries before we found one that took us in. I recall the emergency room only too well. The dirty floor was blood-stained and a torn sheet hung from the bed. Eventually a doctor appeared and after examining Frieda was able to strap her arm tightly against her chest. He administered some painkillers, and we left to make the long, wearisome drive back to Amman. It was evening when we arrived; Mohammad had driven slowly all the way to avoid jolting the damaged arm. Nevertheless, it was still necessary for us to take turns to sit beside Frieda and brace her against any bumps or swerves.

We immediately reported ourselves to the queen, who suggested that Daphne and I go to bed and rest, and then arranged for a doctor to see Frieda. The incident was not referred to again and it was as if we had never been in danger of losing our lives at all.

* * * * *

After twelve years at JTV I began to feel trapped in a system that I didn't really care for, and I had also become rather unwell with increasing blood pressure and headaches. It was not easy to leave: if you left voluntarily you were free to go, but without a bonus for all the years spent there. If you were sacked of course there was nothing. Mr Kamal suggested that I obtain a doctor's certificate which enabled me to leave on health grounds, and that meant I could then claim my twelve-years' bonus. I have always been so grateful to him for this. I walked out of the main gate at JTV in February 1984 with no party, no farewells and I have not set foot inside it again.

What to do now? Alone, jobless, with not much money, I couldn't remain in Jordan non bona fide. Not long afterwards, however, Celia Cawston rang me. She and her husband Tony were here for some years while Tony (a retired lieutenant colonel) worked in Jordan as the representative of British Aerospace. She told me that Tony needed a confidential secretary to work at home with him and keep things running during his frequent absences while he travelled around the Middle East.

Thus began a very pleasant period working with Tony. His office was the floor above their flat, and I often had a quick bite with them before leaving. Tony was an interesting person and a man of many attributes: a barrister, a fluent Arabic speaker, and very knowledgeable on butterflies. In 1985 when my younger stepson, wife and family came out to visit me, the Cawstons most generously gave them the 'office' flat during their stay. My hours were mornings only and this left my afternoons free to begin teaching, but privately. I had learnt from a number of British parents that they wanted extra tuition for their youngsters, in English and occasionally Latin. My expertise lay with children ranging in age from five to nine and, in those early years of teaching, there was a considerable number of boys and girls in need of help. I remember feeling very daring asking for two dinars an hour, but was glad of the money and happy to be back in a milieu I so much enjoyed.

The number of pupils for afternoon lessons slowly increased and so did my fees, particularly when I discovered how much could be charged, but whatever I asked for I believe was fair.

1986 was a happy spring with the visit of my brother Colin. By that time I had, thankfully, moved from the villa into a ground-floor flat which had a garden and central heating, and was much more comfortable. I had also acquired a Honda Civic hatchback named Holly and we could travel around easily. Of course we went to Petra, and I am amazed to think back to the time when I walked in, climbed up to the High Place of Sacrifice, down the long descent the other side, had a quick picnic and then assaulted the track to the Deir, finally walking all the way back to our hotel. The weather that March was perfect, and Colin saw not only fine sites but something of the beautiful flowering countryside.

There was to be another journey that year which came out of the blue. Tim Hackworth had been the Military Attaché in Amman and when he and his wife, Jan, were posted to the British Embassy in Seoul, they offered their friends certain dates to visit them in late spring, the frozen ground having almost thawed. It so happened that Colin had a month's assignment in Hong Kong during May, and I decided to take up the Hackworth's offer and visit them at the beginning of the month. An overnight stopover in Bangkok offered me the chance to see the city again and include newer sites before flying on, first to Taipeh and then to Seoul. Everything in South Korea seemed so well regulated. After the devastating Korean war of the 1950s, the country had been badly torn. The hillsides were laid bare by the ravages of fighting and gunfire with barely a tree in sight. At the end of the conflict, President Pak ordered the entire replanting of every hill with forests of mixed wood trees. This is what I saw all over the country whilst travelling from north to south. Another interesting feature was the complete underground shopping area in Seoul. During the long bitter winters it was hazardous to shop at street level. So there were several floors of shops beneath the pavements, where you could buy everything and anything. By May, boxes of brilliant flowers were arranged in colourful rows on the broad city pavements and outside in the country women arranged their huge pots of kimchee, the pickled cabbages used as a mainstay of the diet throughout the winter months. Most of their dwellings were constructed of wood with round thatched roofs. I watched with interest the start of spring ploughing. Pairs of huge oxen were yolked together to draw the ploughshare through still almost frozen ground, while along the verges sprays of wild iris stood tall beside yellow daisies and other charming flora, all unknown to me. Alas, there was no time to study them as I had to press on.

On a free day Tim kindly took Jan and myself from Seoul all the way up to Panmunjom, the demarcation line between North and South Korea. Here we were instructed by a US Marine sergeant to do exactly as we were told and under no circumstances to stray from the designated pathway. The area of no-man's land between the two Koreas was heavily mined.

Tim took us to 'Gloster Hill' and related how in April 1951 during the Korean War the Gloucester Regiment withstood an overwhelming assault from the Chinese, who had crossed the Imjin River to attack the United Nations forces. Looking across this wasteland to the far mountains of North Korea, I pictured the intense, bitter fighting that had taken place.

On another occasion, we travelled with Tim to Pusan in the far south of the peninsula. The supporting walls of the steeply sloping wooded hillsides were frequently covered with wild yellow jasmine. Preparations were well afoot to celebrate the Buddha's birthday, and everywhere you saw strings of paper lanterns dancing wildly in the breeze. Pusan is a major city and a vast port. The wide stone jetties were packed with fishmongers, many of them women. Seated on the ground, they displayed their wares in round handwoven baskets filled with fish of every kind – with or without their heads, which latter could be sold in quantity if desired. Haggling always took place while choosing the fish, but once that was settled and the fish wrapped in newspaper, the deal was done. I longed to take pictures, but had strained my back and was only able to shuffle along, often slipping on blood and intestines.

While Tim attended his meetings Jan and I drove to the war cemetery. This had been set up to commemorate the fallen of the 1950–1953 Korean War. The result is a beautifully designed resting place for those of every nation who fought in this savage conflict. Here lie the remains of 11,000 men of the United Nations Forces who fell over that period. The British soldiers are buried on the grassy slope and each grave bears their name or, if unknown, the simple words, 'Known unto God'.

I bid 'Farewell' to Korea and 'Hello' to Hong Kong. Colin had booked me into a hotel not far from his military establishment and during the day, while he was working, I explored on foot. I went up to the Peak (1,800 feet), enjoyed the views and much appreciated its temperate climate in contrast to the tropical heat at sea level. I travelled on to Stanley, where history records the last stand of the British and Canadian troops before surrender to the Japanese in 1941. Later I explored the harbour at Aberdeen, which I found to be messy, dirty and extremely smelly. The large Chinese junks were all jammed together and their refuse spilled into the water. Nevertheless, the area offered many fish restaurants. I have since learnt that the authorities undertook a massive cleaning campaign and a number of the junks were ordered outside the harbour. Colin and I took a hover-craft to Macau, then still a Portuguese possession. It was a strange place, and nothing like the glamourous gaming resort I had expected to find. We walked along a causeway to enter the city, passing the ruined façade of a once beautiful cathedral. The streets were untidy, with broken pavements and many of the shops were boarded up. Old Portuguese houses stood neglected in overgrown gardens, quite often filled with shallow pools of stagnant oily water. There was little sign of bustle in the shopping district and we could not even find a café in which to quench our thirst. I felt Macau had reached the end of its time amongst the fleshpots. A few years later it was handed back to China.

* * * * *

In December 1987 the Cawstons and another family arranged a trip along the Nile for a week just prior to Christmas. I was to look after the 'shop'. Then, suddenly, Celia called me two days before their departure to ask if I would like to join them. Would I! There was a race to see if a spare cabin still existed. It did. Could I afford the cost of everything? Just about. Passport, money, quick packing of clothes, of course my camera, and I was ready.

We flew into Cairo at night and stayed in a comfortable hotel until our early morning flight to Luxor. The 'Isis' was moored near Karnak and we had the advantage of going aboard, unpacking, and then having the rest of the day to sightsee before the arrival of the other passengers.

The weather was balmy and everything well watered and green as we strolled the one kilometre to the ruins of Karnak. It is without doubt one of the most stunning places I have ever seen. The entrance to it is lined with forty ram-headed sphinxes, each with a miniature Rameses II standing between their paws. We entered the temple of Rameses III and then went on into the Great Hypostyle Hall. This appeared to me as a giant 'forest'. Each of the 134 massive sand-coloured pillars stands 69 feet high with a circumference of 33 feet. You have to lean backwards and still crane your neck to see their circular capitals. They are so magnificent and over-powering, yet immensely beautiful. Every column depicts the traditional pattern of pharaohs honouring their gods in processions and scenes. It was entertaining to use our simplified code on hieroglyphics and decipher some of the patterns. It is worth visiting Luxor just to see Karnak alone.

Later we returned to view the temple complex of Amun in the modern town of Luxor and were duly awed by the colossal twin statues of Rameses II at the main entrance. The impressive inner sanctuary was rebuilt by Alexander the Great.

With a full complement of passengers that evening, we all met, introduced ourselves and enjoyed an excellent buffet. This was the pattern for meals throughout the voyage and it worked very well. Our Nubian crew were so friendly and jolly that even without a language to share, we communicated easily.

The boat remained overnight at Luxor and the next day we crossed the Nile by ferry to the Valley of the Kings (Thebes) and spent the day viewing some of the tombs. I am not greatly interested in archaeology and have a limited capacity for absorbing dates or raving over bits of pottery or layers of varying rock strata, often more attracted by the small 'asides' such as a donkey drawing a load of mud bricks, small grubby, barefoot children with a young kid, or an elderly Egyptian displaying the ancient art of engraving and painting pictures on clay. Having said that, I was immensely impressed by the stature and beauty of many of the great temples.

Before returning across the river to Luxor we stopped to look at the Colossi of Memnon, two isolated statues over 3,000 years old. We sailed downriver during that night, awoke to a cool, misty dawn and tied up near the great Graeco-Roman ruins at Dendarah. Massive and most impressive they were, even in their decayed state. The Roman sanctuary with its five columns and beautifully decorated capitals of palm leaves and lotus flowers is part of the temple complex. I was particularly intrigued and awed not only by the countless wall reliefs depicting pharaonic gods like Horus, but also an engraving of King Ptolemy wearing the double crown of Upper Egypt. He was Cleopatra's son by Caesar.

The sun was well risen and the chill of early morning had dissipated as we took a bus and drove away from the river, but alongside a canal towards Abydos. On this drive we were able to see a little more of Egypt's rural landscape. There were fields of sugar cane, much already cut and borne away on heavily laden camels. Near the water's edge stood simple straw-thatched dwellings with children, buffaloes, ducks and geese all crowded together in the muddy shallows. The youngsters were colourfully dressed: orange, red, green and shocking pink predominating. This was in sharp contrast to the womenfolk who all wore black from top to bottom. They were a cheerful lot, clapping, dancing and shouting as the bus passed by.

And so to Abydos, one of the oldest cities of Ancient Egypt, and notable for the memorial temple of Seti I, which contains an amazing inscription from the nineteenth dynasty known as the Abydos King List.

When not ashore, it was so pleasant and relaxing to go up on deck and watch the shoreline slip by. Early morning sunlight brought the cream and white painted houses sharply into focus as they nestled beneath the shade of tall date palms. On one occasion we were attracted by noise overhead and, looking up, saw a group of pelicans flying by. They passed so low that we could note their brown colour and smaller size than those of the large white species. I loved the evenings of breathtaking sunsets followed by the soft glow on the river, and the appearance of small fishing craft. Since time immemorial the fishermen have cast their nets. From a distance, they looked like giant spiders' webs, glistening with drops of water. Quite magical.

We went ashore again at Esna. Here the temple complex was much closer to the town, and we mingled with the local shoppers, donkey carts laden with sacks of flour or clay bricks, children scurrying all around or just stopping to stare at us. And, as always, the call to buy was ever present.

At Edfu the Graeco-Roman temple is well preserved and lies between Kom Ombo and Esna. Dedicated to the god Horus (the falcon), it forms part of a huge courtyard.

Our final destination was Aswan where we said a warm and grateful farewell to the crew. Throughout the voyage we had received such willing and kindly service. The Egyptian captain had allowed us to join him, one at a time, in the tiny wheelhouse, much of the space being taken up by his portly self.

Aswan is the last port on the Nile before entering the cataracts and thence to the mighty southern barrage of the Aswan Dam. The river runs through a deep gorge, the cliffs rising vertically some 100 feet, on the top of which stands the town itself. Our hotel, the Old Cataract, was a very long, handsome structure built in terracotta stone and a one-time summer palace of King Farouk, the last Egyptian monarch. I was struck by the number of staircases leading to the first and second floors, and frequently took the wrong one. Everything was on a vast scale, and my bedroom and bathroom alone would have been accommodation for a family living in a modest bungalow! We intended only to spend one night there, but so enjoyed the place that we extended it to two and cut out a last night in Cairo.

Rising early next morning, I wandered around the garden and was immediately taken back to memories of my youth in pre-war India. The gardener had just finished watering the plants and, as I smelt that special freshness of earth and water, I had some moments of great nostalgia, remembering most vividly the wonderful public garden in

17. At almost five kilometres, the Bangabundhu Bridge spans the Jamuna river, connecting northern Bangladesh to India. March 1998

18. Jute sellers in Tangail, northern Bangladesh 1997

19. Timeless living: Women washing clothes at Muktagacha, Bangladesh.

20. A craftsman repairing an old Turkish carpet, Istanbul 1999

21. Fish for sale! The lit bulbs hung to keep flies at bay, Istanbul 1999

22. Istanbul, Aya Sophia, 1999

23. Entrance into the ruins
of Babylon, Iraq 1999

24. Unloading Canadian
wheatflour into the Red Crescent
warehouse at Karbala, 1999

25. Members of the Mennonite Central Committee team in the courtyard of the Mosque of Hussein at Karbala, 1999. The visit was part of their aid programme for Iraq.

26. Craftsmen at work in the Copper Souq, Baghdad 1999

27. The main door of the Duomo
façade, Florence 2000

28. Flowery balconies by the Ponte Vecchio, Florence

29. Jerusalem. A welcome mid-morning break during the Ecumenical Forum, 2002

30. Palm Sunday, Jerusalem, 13th April 2003. *Left to right:* Archbishop of Canterbury, Rowan Williams, Ann, Bishop Riah Abu Al Assal, Rev. Yazeed Said (Acting Dean)

31. Wedding of Johnny and Jenny, Shelburne, Vermont, 9ᵗʰ August 2003

32. Engagement of Harry and Christina, Cranborne 2004

33. My good friend Diane on an archaeological trip near Wadi Ibn Hammad, Jordan

34. Transfering washed phosphate from a tipper at the Al-Abiad Mine, Jordan 2007

35. A dragline at the Al-Hassa Mine clearing the overburden to expose the phosphate

36. Loading a cargo ship with phosphate at the JPMC jetty, Aqaba 2007

Jullundur, where so many similar flowers grew. The paths and beds were edged exactly the same way, with white-washed bricks laid at an angle, forming a long zigzag. Looking at this pretty place, I might have been right back there.

From the hotel we had fine views down to the river towards the few small cataracts which flow below the Aswan Dam. Otherwise the water ran smoothly but with a strong current. Of course we took a sail, or should I say, glide, in a felucca which was slow enough to enjoy looking at life by the water's edge, but always with the possibility that we might collide with another felucca. They are rather cumbersome and rely totally on their single large white sail. Later we drove to Lake Nasser, really a mini sea several hundred kilometers long, to admire the giant structure of the Aswan Dam itself.

Finally, we took a flight back to Cairo and on to Amman, but not before we had spent some fascinating hours at the Museum of Egyptian Antiquities. We only had time to explore the wonders of the Pharaonic period of Tutankhamun, which occupied an entire floor. Arriving back in Amman two days before Christmas, there was little time for reflection until after the festive season. Of all my travel holidays, I rate this very highly.

11

I continued working for Tony until the advent of the computer. I could type and had mastered the telex and, later, fax machines but had never touched a computer. Fortunately, the wife of the British Defence Attaché was well acquainted with them and we had a smooth handover. I had much enjoyed working with Tony, meeting a lot of high-ranking Jordanian officers and being the recipient of much kindness from Celia.

There was a growing demand for studying English, especially amongst the expatriate community. Many of them had children who needed to study in English while in Jordan, and I gave private lessons to the younger ones of many nationalities. Among the most rewarding were Japanese, Russians, French, a Jordanian and a Brazilian. Little Keiko – knee-high to a grasshopper – was only five and a half when her mother brought her, and I had to place three cushions on the chair for her to see what she was doing. She knew no word of English, and being left alone with a middle-aged, white-haired lady could have seemed daunting, but not at all. Keiko was a bundle of enthusiasm and very quick. I recall her bouncing up and down on her chair saying, 'I love learning!' And learn she did, very fast. Within only a few weeks she had mastered the alphabet, the basic vowel sounds and as for her writing, it was quite beautiful. Her favourite subject was reading and her parents were extremely helpful in buying her many of the books I suggested. I also taught one or two Japanese boys. They, too, worked diligently, but unlike Keiko, were very hesitant to speak, always afraid of making a mistake. I guess that is part of Japanese culture. In contrast, their written work was meticulous.

Then there were my two Russian girls. One was a daughter of the manager of Aeroflot, the other the only child of the representative of Ita Tass. They could not have been more different: Tania was small, slim, neat in dress and, in due course, always neat with her work; Vera was tall for her age, extremely pretty with wide Slavic features, vivid blue eyes and gorgeous thick, corn-coloured hair plaited in a single long pigtail. Vera was a delightful child, but with little wish to study.

They came together for lessons and in the early sessions I had one each side of me while I read a simple story and asked them to follow the words. Tania took her studies seriously and really wanted to learn. Young Vera, a precious child of mature parents would snuggle up to me, often with a kiss and say she found it too difficult. So I had to start splitting the lessons into separate work for each, and Tania soon raced ahead. They were both very lithe, studying ballet and gymnastics in true Russian fashion and, when trying to explain something to me about those classes, would suddenly leave the table and do splits or arch their backs so their hands and feet touched the floor.

About nine months later, Vera stopped coming and returned with her parents to Moscow. I missed her charm and warmth, and am glad to have a lovely picture of the two of them taken on an outing when we picnicked with friends, and they met a shepherd who let them hold a kid.

I think Tania was rather relieved when Vera left. She and I settled down to an excellent progression of work which we both enjoyed. More importantly, her parents were equally enthusiastic and interested in their daughter's progress and, in due course, I took her younger sister, Katia. Two years on and sadly they had to leave, but I felt Tania was well able to cope with her school in Russia. I received a very fine reference from her father.

There was also a small French contingent. Out of the blue, strangers would ring the bell and ask if, or rather when, I could start tutoring their child. The three Petrie boys were living in Amman with their French mother, France, while her husband was working in Gaza. I taught the elder two, Arthur and Oliver – Arthur serious, hardworking and very French; Oliver an Anglophile who much preferred speaking in English and had a light-hearted approach to study. Regretfully, the parents began to split up, and finally France had no option but to leave Jordan and go back to France. We kept in touch for a good while.

Last but far from least was Mariana, whose father held a senior position within the Brazilian Embassy in Amman. Aged four and nine months, she was already attending the International Community School in Amman, but had informed her mother that she was bored. She came to me twice a week and I don't think I have ever taught such a highly intelligent and interesting child of that age. She just devoured her work and had a strong will, but was so amusing and full of laughter, it was bliss to have her. She loved everything she did and, like so many foreign youngsters, had to start English from scratch. In no time she mastered the letters and sounds, and adored reading and writing. I was amazed at the tidiness of her work and mastery of pencil. She copied very exactly the manner of joining letters, punctuation and the refinements of any written sentences. Alas, after only a brief time in Amman, her father's position was upgraded (I was not surprised), and the family left at short notice for Vienna. I only had Mariana for six months, but it is my hope that she forged ahead and will become a fine academic star.

If I have not mentioned any Jordanian students so far, it is because they were on the whole by far the most difficult. The majority were boys and, in many cases, came from privileged backgrounds with charming, cultured parents. But the common thread running amongst them all, boys and girls, was a lack of discipline. They frequently arrived late and had often not done their homework. Their attention span was short and they were so easily diverted. Much of my teaching was what I would call 'patching up' – that is, trying to give them the basic grounding so seemingly lacking then in private schools. With their school studies as well, it was hard for both pupil and teacher to do this. Alas, the absence of that vital basic teaching at a young age can hardly ever be made up.

Young Karim came to me, his delightful Spanish mother at her wits' end to know what to do with him. The youngest of three boys with his father working in Iraq, it fell to mum to keep things going. She had hired a male tutor for Karim that summer, but the man lasted only a short while before packing it in. So when he came to me in the autumn, I was a little prepared for a difficult child. Extremely bright and talkative, but totally disinclined to apply himself, he set out to be as obstructive as possible. That is, until one afternoon I told him to put down his pencil and listen to me. In a few pithy, stinging sentences I told him exactly what I thought of him and gave him two options. We sat in silence for a while (hopefully the pressure of that was suitably unnerving) and then he said he wanted to work.

I immediately changed my tone of voice back to normal as if nothing had happened, and we continued where we had left off. I never raised the subject again and indeed had no need to. From that day on I had a lovely, lively boy to work with and he just flew through his work as well as becoming cheerful, nice-mannered and very keen. I rate Karim as one of my successes and one of my star pupils.

The years rolled on and I continued teaching full-time. With a regular income, I had the leisure to take up again my ever-growing interest in Jordan's flora. Having acquired a fine camera in Switzerland, I was now able to use my macro lens and obtain much better images. I was encouraged by friends to make cards, which I sold at the RSCN shop. The Royal Society for the Conservation of Nature was the dream of the late Anis Mouasher, a man utterly devoted to Jordan and the preservation of its remarkable heritage. Taking close-up pictures of flowers in situ, I then had them printed and inserted each picture into a quality card. Providing both English and botanical names was also important in each case. These proved to be a 'first' in Jordan, and for many years I sold them not only to the RSCN but to other outlets.

As my knowledge grew, so did the need to travel further afield. I took my car and camera on exciting explorations, often without any idea of the outcome. Fortunately, I have a good sense of direction and soon began to learn the lie of the land. I came to know where the earliest cyclamen flowered, where the finest quality anemones and red buttercups were to be found, or to look in Dibeen Woods for dainty orchids. Of course, one must not forget the black iris. How many times have I been asked, 'Where can we find the black iris?' Following on from my flower photography, I launched into taking some of the numerous beautiful sites and scenes of Jordan. This led to an occasional photographic exhibition where I not only hoped to sell the pictures, but could enthuse and encourage viewers to go out and see all these places for themselves.

* * * * *

At the beginning of the crisis arising from Iraq's invasion of Kuwait in 1990, many foreign families and embassy staff were obliged to leave Jordan, among them my friend Reinfriede Ilker, whose husband was an agricultural expert working with US Aid. Rather than travel all the way back to the United States, they opted to go to Cyprus where Hikmat could set up an office and continue his plant studies. They kindly suggested that after things had quietened down I might like a break in Cyprus. What a great idea! I flew to Larnaca where Reinfriede picked me up and we drove to their flat on the outskirts of Limassol. Cyprus has a long history of invasions and occupations, and I discovered that it was in Limassol that Richard I of England had married Berengaria of Navarre at St. George's Chapel on 12 May, 1191. During the day, while the Ilkers were busy, I took buses to various points along the coast and spent enjoyable hours botanizing by the seashore. At the weekend we hired a car and drove up into the Troodos Mountains and explored the northern part of the Greek side of the island. We drove through a number of abandoned villages, so attractive, even in their emptiness, and I learnt that these had been occupied by Turkish Cypriots before partition. The Ilkers had friends in the UN and one day we walked across no man's land in Nicosia and joined them on the Turkish side to hire a taxi for the day. Since we had to be back in Nicosia by five o'clock it was not possible to see everything in the north. We opted to drive up the western side and thence to the pan handle of San Andreas, stopping anywhere else that might be of interest.

Our first halt across the border was the seaport and ancient city of Famagusta. Here, we were immediately looking at history. From the twelfth century Famagusta began to increase in importance. With a natural harbour and strong walls, it became a haven for the influx of

Christians fleeing the downfall of Acre in 1291. Seized by Genoa in 1372 and later by Venice, considerable commercial activity led to great wealth. From 1570 to 1571 Famagusta held out against the Ottoman siege, but finally surrendered. The city was renowned for its many churches and, although today Islam prevails, only the cathedral has been converted into a mosque.

Just north of Famagusta lies Salamis, with its archaeological finds going back to the Late Bronze Age. In the fifth century BC, Evagoras became ruler of the whole island and won its independence from Persian rule. On his first journey Paul landed here and preached in the synagogues. Several earthquakes led to the city's destruction; most of the extant ruins date from the Roman period. I found the place very unusual, especially since much of the ancient city lies under the sea and can be seen by wading into the shallows and peering through the translucent water. The weather was hot and the atmosphere peaceful, with just the sound of cicadas and the gentle lapping of the waves.

We continued right up to the extreme easterly point of the island to the monastery of San Andreas before driving along the sandy northern coast. The seascapes were beautiful, much of the land unoccupied. When passing through villages and towns, however, I was struck by the overall order and cleanliness. The Turkish shopkeepers were very friendly and we enjoyed Turkish kebabs and dolmas (stuffed vine leaves). On the way back to Nicosia we were stopped by a farmer. One of his sheep had just been struck by a car. Our driver immediately offered to take it off his hands and loaded the dying animal into the boot. Of course the poor thing died, but on arrival in Nicosia, the driver immediately opened the boot and started negotiating with several interested onlookers for the best sale price. We left him still haggling and could hear the arguments long after we were out of sight.

Reflecting on this first visit to Cyprus, I decided that it would not be a country in which to settle. My overall picture, in particular of Limassol, was of an ever growing concrete jungle with hotels, boarding houses, and apartment blocks crammed along the beautiful sandy beaches. Since the hotels, with their divided strips of beach, were barred except to hotel guests, no access to the shore was available to the ordinary visitor.

* * * * *

With thoughts of travel never far from my mind, in February 1997 I accepted an invitation to stay with old friends from Jordan who were now stationed in Bangladesh. Michael Taylor was constructing a bridge across the Jamuna River. He was the Engineer's Representative responsible for the administration of the bridge contract and also for the site supervision of the contractor for the bridge works. Building a bridge of five kilometres in length across the Jamuna River was a vast project and involved a consortium of consulting engineers – Rendel, Palmer & Tritton (UK), Nedeco from the Netherlands and Bangladesh Consultants. The bridge would carry road, rail, natural gas, high voltage electricity and telecommunications, and would also connect Bangladesh with India.

I arrived at Dhaka Airport early in the morning and can never forget the scene which met my eyes. Looking down from the airport building was a sea of humanity, rickshaws, tuktuks and stray animals, giving a kaleidoscope of colour, with the crescendo of voices soaring above all else. I felt I had come home, and a surge of joy and excitement ran through me. It was almost India – and hopefully that would come one day. Mike and his wife Lotte finally extricated me from the throng and, after a refreshing break, we took to the road for a long drive north.

Our destination was Bhuapur, close to the site workshops and where the Taylors had a house on the expat compound at the Jamuna Bridge Project. The layout was very pleasant with plenty of room between the bungalows. Dutch built and furnished, they were both cool and comfortable. Gardens were full of colour; the most predominant plant not unnaturally being marigolds. There were also roses, zinnias, cannas and sweet scented shrubs, as well as brilliant bougainvillea.

I was absolutely fascinated by the size of the proposed bridge, and not only that but the immense amount of preparation to be done in the riverbed and along its banks. Bangladesh is a country virtually

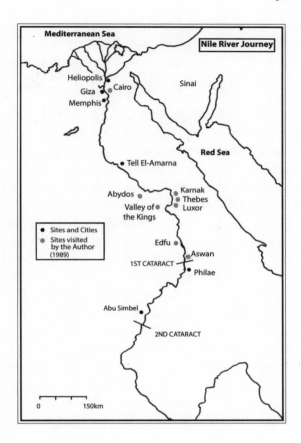

devoid of rock. This entailed massive deliveries of the material to be trucked from India, to build up the banks of the river and give it permanent safety against flooding. There was also the clearance of many sandbanks known as chars. Dredgers pumped the sand through pipes to the shore where it was collected in baskets and loaded into trucks for disposal – a back-breaking and labour intensive operation employing dozens of men.

Much of the workforce was made up of South Koreans. They represented the Hyundai Engineering & Construction Corporation and were contractors for the design and construction of the main bridge. Each span was 100 metres. I watched the work practically from the beginning, and the following year, almost to the day, I went once more to Bhuapur to see this remarkable engineering feat just two spans short of completion. What a thrill! In July 1998 the bridge was officially opened under the name of Bangabandhu.

Apart from the enthralling time watching the bridge construction, Lotte took me to some interesting historical sites. Among them was the very fine *rajbhari* ('royal residence'), at Muktagacha built during the Raj and, although now neglected, still proud standing. I could easily picture life in such a place, with its beautiful gardens, perhaps peacocks on the lawn, and countless servants to ensure the comfort and smooth running of such an establishment. A number of these *rajbharis* are now in good use as teacher training colleges, as we saw in Mymensingh, where a charming group of women students kindly posed for my camera. In another lovely building within the same complex, the original chandelier and etched glass swing doors are still in place. Mymensingh also gave me my first ever glimpse of the mighty Brahmaputra. I learnt that in Buddhism all rivers are considered female. The Brahmaputra is the exception; Brahma being a god, and in Sanskrit, putra meaning son. I had wandered off from my friends, determined to find the river, and standing on the bank I more or less had the place to myself. Across the river stood hectares of jute fields, and immediately below me a boat was being towed by two youths who walked along the bank. One day I hope to see much more of this great waterway.

When I returned to Bangladesh in February 1998, one of the first things that Lotte and I did was to drive into Tangail, the nearest large town. Apart from stopping to look at almost everything, we eventually made our way to one of Lotte's favourite shops. As soon as I saw the open front with a short flight of steps to a platform, I knew this could only be an emporium offering sari material. We settled comfortably on a couple of bolsters and were first served tea. When all was clear, the owner then commenced to pull out and almost drown us with his endless display of breathtaking cottons and silks; every hue, every shade, many sparkling with glitter, others finished in hand stitched floral designs; shot silk purples and midnight blues; gossamer fine cotton shimmering in soft cream or pink. So it went on, by which time I had mentally bought half the shop. We finally came down to earth and between us took a light blue for Lotte and a peacock blue for me.

On another occasion we took the driver and went off to look at history. One memorable site was the Atia Mosque which was built in 1609 and predates the Moghul period. It is remarkable for its superb decorative brickwork, particularly the varying floral scrolls, all on the front façade only. This was quite as beautiful as similar work I had seen in Delhi. I am so glad I have pictures of these bygone gems.

Bangladesh is really a giant flood plain. The rivers, fed by the devastating annual monsoon, regularly flood the flat land, leaving a rich residue of silt behind. This is what gives the padi fields their 'gold' – rice. But at a cost. I learnt that farmsteads and smallholdings, not built high enough above the waterline, are simply washed away each year. The many brickworks dotted about the rural areas suffer the same fate. Brickmaking is an important localized industry, providing material for constant road repairs as well as the construction of buildings.

To a photographer and nature lover, the brilliance of young green padi at the start of the season is almost unbelievable. The land is formed into giant plots, each with a *bund* or raised bank to enclose the water into which the seedlings are placed. It must be back breaking work, endlessly bending down to position each small plant.

I saw acres of pineapple for the first time, along with bananas and, of course, giant mango trees in full flower. It is a timeless land governed so much by rainfall and sunshine. Amidst it all live millions of people, the majority in poverty. Watching their simple tasks offered me a chance to take pictures of everyday life. Large stone built water tanks are to be found throughout the villages, shaded by tall trees. Each village will replicate another – groups of chattering women, colourful in their brilliant saris, squatting on the steps at the water's edge with the family washing. I watched black pigs rooting in dry padi fields, and was intrigued by the poles used to hold the fishing nets in numerous backwaters.

On one occasion we stopped to watch the cattle sales. Many animals are brought in from India and sold as ploughing teams. Then there are the people! I never saw any town or village except as a constant swirling, shouting, jostling body of humanity. With a cacophony of bells, each cycle rickshaw miraculously avoided another, all the while, the occupants remaining quietly seated. Cows, sacred to Hindus, often lay in the middle of the street, placidly ignoring the human throngs. Pi dogs scratched themselves or hunted for something to eat in the garbage piled at the roadside. Beggars, too, abounded and it was generally impossible for me to descend from the car for fear of being totally engulfed. On the larger roads it was first come, although if you were facing an oncoming bus it was essential to drive at least halfway off the road – the buses did not reduce speed or attempt any other position except the centre.

On my last day, Mike took Lotte and me by launch right across the Jamuna where I could see preparation for the placing of the final two spans of the Bangabandhu Bridge.

* * * * *

It was many years since I had been to Turkey, so in 1999 I was delighted to accept an invitation from an old friend, Anne Sears. She and her husband, John, had been in Jordan for a while during the construction of the Karameh Dam in the Jordan Valley. They had lived in a condominium near the site. Anne was a fine artist and we held a joint exhibition at the British Council in Amman, she with her paintings and I with my photographs. Princess Basma had very graciously opened it and both Anne and I had sold quite a number of our exhibits.

At the beginning of April 1999, I flew to Istanbul for a week packed with interest. We spent much time in and around the old city. Although I had lived and worked in Turkey, it was a joy to have the leisure to saunter again through the bazaar, and to revisit the Aya Sophia, built by Justinian and dedicated in 537 AD, and the superb

'Blue Mosque' with its six minarets, built and completed by Sultan Ahmed in 1617. We watched carpet mending, in the traditional manner using only natural dyed wools, and I took pictures of the colourful display of rugs. On into Topkapı to admire Aya Irene; at one time a cathedral and never converted into a mosque, it is now an exhibition hall. In a cobbled street close by we discovered some newly restored wooden houses with pretty façades; I certainly wouldn't have minded living in one myself. In the Spice Market there were intriguing displays of seeds and spices, dried roots and nuts. Fish was also temptingly laid out, above it hanging lit bulbs. I can only guess that they were used as a form of deterrent to flies and other insects.

When I had first lived and worked in Turkey, it had been on the Anatolian side of the Bosphorus, in Asia Minor. Now I was viewing it from 'Europe' as it were, and Anne and I wandered down to the waterfront at Eminönü near the Galata Bridge to look at the fishing smacks and watch the ferries plying in and out as they crossed to the opposite shore or travelled further south into the Sea of Marmara. We even partook of a fish sandwich. On our final visit to the sea we took the ferry to Üsküdar. That trip had such memories for me. Many a time I had crossed over there before continuing in a dolmuş (servis taxi) to Moda. Formerly known as Scutari, Üsküdar was made famous by Florence Nightingale who had nursed at the British Military hospital during the Crimean War.

One day, John took time off from work and we drove up the European side, heading north along the Bosphorus. We lunched at an excellent fish restaurant overlooking the sea where you could watch the shipping. Timber carriers passed slowly by coming from the Black Sea, and a gigantic oil tanker, escorted by two tugs, made its ponderous way in the opposite direction. By now the sky had darkened dramatically as dense fog descended and our view was almost obliterated. (Navigation aids are vital on this incredibly busy maritime channel.) It had been a delightful few days only marred by an unannounced six-hour wait at the airport for my return flight.

12

Back in Amman on, I hastened to prepare for yet another journey, this one to Baghdad. I had always been interested in Iraq ever since learning of my father's time serving there in the 1920s. He had visited Kurdistan, and I recall how warmly he spoke of the people and their way of life. He had also learnt of their political aspiration for an independent state within Iraq. Now, years later, following several very serious conflicts between Iraq and Iran between 1980 and 1988, Iraq's invasion of Kuwait in 1990 and the Gulf War of 1991, a number of humanitarian organizations had been working in the country. One of these, MCC (Mennonite Central Committee), was based in Amman, and their representatives, Greg and Fay Foster, travelled to Iraq from time to time to follow up on the work being done by their Iraqi colleagues. The Fosters told me that if I could obtain a visa from Baghdad they would take me on their next eight-day visit. I did obtain it, and on 15th April we set off – by road, there being no flights. We travelled in a comfortable eight-seater bus, well equipped with bottle holders and a system for heating coffee, for the eleven-hour journey. At Ruwaished, the Jordan/Iraq border crossing, we handed in our paperwork and got out to stretch our legs. There is a duty-free shop and, whiling away the time, I saw and bought a steam iron – something I had never had. Fay wisely suggested I pay for it and leave it there until our return, which I did.

Leaving the border we entered utterly dreary country, driving for miles and miles across the Badiet esh Sham (Syrian Desert), only occasionally passing through clusters of dwellings. It was not until many hours later when we crossed the Euphrates that the landscape changed dramatically. This time it was mile upon mile of tall, dusty, dark green date palms, almost as monotonous as the desert. We were nearing Baghdad, however, and finally drew up at the Hamra Hotel, our home for the next few days.

I had, of course, brought my camera, but was quite aware of the restrictions likely to be imposed on its use. In any case, Greg gave me stark warning about particularly sensitive areas along the river or near any barracks or soldiery. Looking at my photographs now, I realize that I did manage to obtain some interesting shots.

One of the main objects of the trip was to visit a number of schools and dispense school bags for the children. These had been made by American children and then filled with scholastic requirements such as pencils, a rubber, ruler, notepad, colouring book and crayons. Visiting these establishments we at once realized how desperately they were needed. Classrooms were stark, devoid of desks or blackboard, the windows with shattered glass or nothing at all. With only a chair or two for the lucky few, the rest sat on the floor. Far from appearing low-spirited, however, these youngsters were amazing. Excited to see us, they crowded round the gifts and laughingly showed us their tiny pencil stumps. We felt humbled and ashamed.

Another day took us to the railway station, or the remains of it. A vast warehouse had been erected close by, and inside it housed an assortment of medicines and foodstuffs awaiting distribution. This was an important part of our mission, and arrangements were made for several trucks to drive to Karbala where the Red Crescent would oversee their delivery to outlying villages and other rural areas. After Arab coffee at the Red Crescent centre in Karbala, we went outside to watch the unloading of the flour trucks.

Karbala is of both historic and religious significance to Muslims. Imam Hussein was the grandson of the prophet Mohammad. He had refused to pledge allegiance to the Umayyad caliph Yazid and fled his hometown of Medina. He was ambushed, killed and beheaded in 680 AD on his way to be with the people of Kufa, near Karbala. In his memory a shrine was built at Karbala. After leaving the Red Crescent offices as well as visiting a makeshift children's hospital, we were all allowed entry into the vast courtyard of the mosque – not before we women had removed our shoes and donned an all-enveloping black chadour which covered us from head to toe. The material for these garments was made of nylon. It was not only very hot, being April, but the material was extremely slippery. This meant that we were constantly using both hands to keep the garment around us. With my camera clutched underneath all this, we had fits of giggles whilst I pushed the lens out of the folds to attempt a picture – which was allowed. The mosque, dating back to the eleventh century, has had several additions and is highly decorated. We had one final act to perform before leaving the area and that was a visit to the Imam. Our guide took us across the courtyard to enter a small austere room and there we three lined up in utter silence seated against a cool wall. Of course, the Imam addressed no word to us or even looked in our direction, and we were hard put not to start laughing again. After the men had exchanged the usual pleasantries, we left and thankfully handed in our borrowed garments before taking the road to Babylon some 85 kilometres south of Baghdad.

Babylon! 'What will it conjure up?' I asked myself. History, drama, songs – all of these? The reality was rather different. Founded some 4,000 years ago, Babylon was the capital of many Mesopotamian dynasties, reaching prominence as the capital city of Babylonia with its second king, Nebuchadnezzar, in the seventh century BC. It was he who planned most of the buildings, few of which remain today. What we saw as we wandered along corridors between high brick walls is mostly reconstruction. There seemed to be endless passages with steps up and down leading into vast roofless chambers. In one such chamber, Alexander the Great died in 323 BC, having planned to restore Babylon to its former glory. I saw the massive Lion of Babylon, carved in basalt, the symbol of Ishtar, goddess of Babylon. It stands alone on an empty plot, but behind on a hill is the vast palace Saddam Hussein built for himself. With the arrival of US tanks during the invasion of 2003, the area was again subjected to damage.

On another occasion we drove 32 kilometres out of Baghdad to look at the ruins of Ctesiphon. Built in the second century BC by the Parthian Persians, it stands on the north east bank of the Tigris. The archway was part of a great banqueting hall and is the widest single span vault in the world. It survived the disastrous flooding of the Tigris in 1887 when much of the building was destroyed. I wish we had had more time to explore here.

Of a far more sobering nature was our time spent at Amiriya, a suburb of Baghdad. Here, on 13th February 1991, two bombs pierced the air raid shelter. More than 380 people died, many of them children. What added to the horror was the bursting of the hot water tanks. The boiling water simply gushed out, scalding many to death. I have pictures of the hole made by the bombs, beneath which is a tangle of twisted steel bars. The site is now a memorial where you can enter the chamber, walk beside the walls and see with your own eyes the imprint of skinned hands.

Our last visit was to the coppersmith's souq, with utensils of every style and shape, water jugs, fluted trays, hanging plates, coffee pots and many unidentifiable, attractive items. There was a constant sound of hammer on metal as the craftsmen beat out old copper into new pieces. The narrow passageway was bulging with humanity, and so colourful. Of course there were innumerable prayer rugs and camel bags hanging from rows of metal hooks, and the makers of Turkish coffee did a brisk trade. I would have liked a camel rug, but was restricted by limited funds. Instead, in an 'antique' shop I bought a lovely green glass goblet. A pair was on offer, but foolishly I only opted for the one and have regretted it ever since. They were Russian made and had probably travelled considerably in time and distance.

In the evenings we sometimes took a taxi into the main streets of Baghdad. Like most of the civilian vehicles in Iraq, taxis were just about running on four wheels. With no possibility of obtaining any replacements or new parts, you were not surprised that the doors had incomplete handles, springs poked into your posteriors and many windscreens had shattered glass. The roads were wide and the pavements generous. The city must have been very beautiful. Clothing, plastic toys, packets of sweets, concertina postcards of bygone days, paper flowers, pots and pans, you name it, were all laid out, and all at dirt cheap prices. We took some negatives into a photographer's and they printed several reels of film for JD5 (about five pounds sterling). The vendors were so pleasant and affable – incredible when you think of what Western nations had done to them.

We returned to Jordan by the same route and I remembered to collect my duty-free iron at the Ruwaished border crossing. It continues to serve me faithfully.

* * * * *

In 2000, together with Colin and Anne, I celebrated my seventieth birthday sightseeing in Tuscany. Apart from travelling through Italy, this was my first proper visit, and you can imagine the delightful hours we spent in Florence and Pistoia. We drove through olive clad hillsides to Vinci, Leonardo's home town. I was interested to note how the trees were pruned. The emphasis appeared to be on creating wide spaces between the main branches, in complete contrast to the 'bushiness' of Jordanian olive trees. I loved Sienna in particular, and also Lucca, even though it was raining heavily there. Colin was a great walker, and together we three took ourselves high up into the hills one day. Parts reminded me of Switzerland, the pastures glowing with wild flowers and the scent of newly cut hay hanging on the breeze. From the summit we had a magnificent view across the lower slopes to meadows and villages strung far below.

* * * * *

As a member of the English speaking congregation of the Anglican Church in Amman and the lay representative, I had for several years attended the annual Church Synod held in Jerusalem. At the beginning of September 2002, I joined a gathering of young theologians who had been invited to attend a conference in Jerusalem under the patronage of Bishop Riah. The conference was aimed at encouraging young Palestinian thinkers to converse theologically and critically. The bishop considered that this was an important way in which to maintain the Christian presence in Palestine and Israel.

During the course of the conference, we made several visits. The first was to Bethlehem and the Church of the Nativity, and then to the new YMCA at Beit Sahour. This was followed by a lively question and answer session at the Lutheran Christmas Church. Here several young people expressed differing opinions on whether or not to remain in Palestine. Some felt strongly that there was nothing to keep them and were quite bitter about a lack of awareness from outside. They were longing to be free. Others were extremely positive and felt equally strongly how important it was to stay.

Next day we went to Ramallah. The town had been under curfew, and it was touch-and-go whether the Israel Defense Forces (IDF) was going to lift it. There we met some of the local congregation before continuing to the Evangelical and Episcopal Home and School for boys and girls, many of them orphaned. Curfew was reimposed the following day with the assault on Yasser Arafat's headquarters.

Last, but far from least, was our visit to Gaza. After clearance through the Eres checkpoint, we were transported in three hospital buses into Gaza City. This tour gave us a brief but shocking insight into the terrible damage done to this once beautiful city: so much rubble from bombed and rocketed buildings, broken furniture and bedding hanging from blasted windows and gaping walls, unpaved rutted streets deep in dust, and dozens of shuttered shops. The people's courage and tenacity remains unbroken, and with it also anger.

We walked through the ruins of Arafat's headquarters and lunched right on the sea. The crystal clear water and perfect sand hide such tragedy; on the horizon lurked an Israeli gunboat. Our final stop was at the Gaza YMCA. There we met and talked with youth leaders and learnt something of their thoughts and hopes, their longings and indomitable determination to continue building and rebuilding for the future.

* * * * *

Summer 2003 was a special year for the family. My nephew Johnny had gained his MA at St Andrews in 2000, and during that time had met Jenny Land, an American from Vermont. He travelled out to the States several times over the next couple of years, and in August 2003 all the Mackenzies flew out there for the wedding. Johnny and Jenny were married in a rural setting; in fact it was a part of the Land's large garden. I was pleasantly surprised by Vermont. With no high rise buildings, the majority of houses were of clapboard construction, often with attractive gardens alongside tree-lined roads. The town of Burlington set an almost sedate pace with its neat shops and remarkably quiet roads, little of the hustle and noise one would expect to find.

We all spent a most enjoyable few days travelling around the state through beautiful, peaceful countryside. Johnny and Jenny are still teaching at St. Johnsbury Academy and now have twin daughters, Lila and Kate.

No sooner had we recovered from the excitement of 2003 than Christina and Harry announced their engagement in the summer of 2004. Harry Dunlop had been an assistant trainer at Newmarket with his godfather, Henry Cecil. Christina had an interesting job in the same town, working as assistant to the chief of the Racing Bureau. They chose to get married that November when flat racing would be over for the season. All planning arrangements were put into top gear. It was such fun, with many village friends offering their help or expertise. The lovely Cranborne church was filled with flowers when they were married on 20th November.

Harry and Christina, with sons Tom and William, now live in Lambourn, where Harry manages an active and successful yard.

* * * * *

The last child I taught was Katherina, another Russian girl who attended the Russian School in Amman, but how different from Tania and Katia! Very much an only child, it distressed me a lot to observe how inordinately possessive and protective her mother was. Her father, the Russian Defence Attaché, was a charming man, and he and Katherina were close. He brought her each time and collected her too. I noticed how he always held her workbag, and on leaving me she would hand it to him. One day, I suggested that at ten years old she was big enough to carry it herself, and so she did, but on the rare occasions that her mother came she literally took over Katherina, with admonishments about keeping warm and putting on a garment even if the child didn't want it.

Katherina was intelligent, but so often hesitant and slow to speak. I found her personality seemed to run on one level only. She didn't express surprise, amusement or even understanding until I asked her several times for an opinion. My feeling grew that she was mentally dominated by her mother. Something was very wrong somewhere but the parents were not forthcoming, and her mother certainly did not welcome my observations about Katherina, however tactfully I expressed them. The child was often absent, and the slightest suggestion of a cold or cough stopped her coming.

Finally, at the end of the summer break, with no word from the parents, I called her father and told him I thought there was no point in continuing. Shortly after that, I learnt that Katherina and her mother had returned again to Russia for good, leaving the Colonel here.

* * * * *

Now free of students, I had to find a way to make up the monetary shortfall. Early in November 2006, I received a phone call from the secretary at the Jordan Phosphate Mines Company. Would I come and see her. Intrigued, I did just that and met Reem, the office manager for Mr Walid Kurdi, the Chairman and CEO of JPMC.

The company had recently been denationalized and, with a new man at the helm, many changes were taking place. The office wanted me to take responsibility for the design and printing of all the new stationery that would now be required. So it was that I moved into an entirely unknown world. I was familiar with photographic production, but this was a challenge, working among business people and getting to grips with the different requirements of many. Logo, paper, colour, headings, business cards, carrier bags and company wrapping paper were just some of the demands. Oh! Yes, and a calendar for 2006.

In March 2007 I was asked if I would like to travel south and photograph specific aspects of the three phosphate mines, together with the fertilizer complex at Aqaba. I was thrilled at the invitation, but also rather apprehensive of the challenge. After all, I had never ventured into such photographic fields and had only my trusty manual Yashica. Like most of us, I was extremely ignorant of the workings of these mines except to know that they were open cast and very extensive.

Reem briefed me well, with the names and contact numbers of the mine managers, and arranged luxury accommodation throughout the trip, including two nights in Petra as well as an overnight stay in Aqaba.

So, armed with a dozen films, notebook, camera and binoculars, I set off early in a comfortable four-wheel drive vehicle together with driver Saleh and escort Imad, both from the JPMC stable and both quite excellent. They had little English so it was good practice as well as fun to make the effort at Arabic conversation, and we got along famously with many a laugh.

About 100 kilometres south we made our first stop, at the oldest of the mines, the Al-Abiad (which means white). In use since the 1930s, it extends eastward, far into the desert. The drive was the easy part. Now I had to meet the mine manager and his colleagues. As a visitor, I shook hands with all and we sat down – to silence. Being the only woman I was outnumbered, and since Arab men are not given to small talk, especially to a woman, I knew I must start the ball rolling. So I started by asking obvious questions like the number of workers, amount of phosphate mined annually, to where it was shipped, and so on. As the replies came back, it gave me time to prepare and phrase the next question. After the usual cup of Turkish coffee, I was introduced to the mine's geologist, who thankfully spoke good English, and we set off at high speed in his jeep to 'see the sights!' He asked me what I wanted to see and I replied, 'Everything'.

Visual education I would term it, with pictures at every stop and some new words like 'beneficiation' frequently thrown into the conversation. Gradually I learnt a superficial amount about the mining, grading, washing, cleaning, drying, and eventually the loading of the phosphate into trucks and wagons for transport to Aqaba. Much of the shipment goes to India, but also to Japan, Indonesia and Brunei.

Mining is a very dusty business, and I was so fortunate in the day being almost windless with a bright blue sky and beautiful clouds. Returning to the manager's office a little better informed, I thanked him and we left the Al-Abiad to continue on to the Al-Hassa Mine, not too far distant. Here the manager, a Christian from Karak, took me himself on an extensive tour and I saw the phosphate mined a little differently. Slow moving drag lines, which look like cranes, are used to dig into the ground with their scoops. Capable of lifting 60 tons at a time, they are then swung away and emptied out on the ground above, forming a 'cut' or trench. The depth of cut depends on the whereabouts of the phosphate seam. Down below trucks await loading from another machine as the dragline moves slowly on. More pictures, more learning and then we returned to the office for a late lunch.

The men employed are Jordanians, most of whom live with their families on the housing estates. The work at the mines is non-stop with eight-hour shifts round the clock. Each mine has accommodation on site with a recreation room, cinema and surgery.

As the light began to fade, we set off to Petra and stopped on the way for me to take a stunning sunset. I was booked in at the very comfortable Crowne Plaza Resort, which is situated just outside the entrance to the ruins and has a fine view.

Early next morning I was walking through the Siq, a narrow passage with towering rocks either side until it opens up to glimpse the Treasury. Carved in relief by the Nabataeans some twenty centuries ago, it is indeed a wonder of the world. I spent the day walking here and there, not pressured by time or necessity to do anything except of my choice. Late afternoon I joined Saleh and Imad for a drive down Wadi Nimlah (Ant Valley) into Wadi Araba, the wadi which runs alongside the Dead Sea and forms the frontier between Jordan and Israel. A new road for me and one I had wanted to explore, it has been rebuilt along the ancient caravan trail, when camels travelled up and down with people and merchandise. I soon lost count of the innumerable bends down into the valley.

Next day we headed southeast to Wadi Rum, another of my favourite places. Being springtime, I hoped to find some desert plants to record and was lucky to come across the showy broomrape. A parasite feeding on the tamarisk, it has a solid cluster of pink tinged blooms all up the stem. There were the usual tall yellow fennels, low white desert campions and the dainty dark-eyed geranium. Rum is a huge place and it is easy to find exciting shots of the mountains, with sand in shades of red, yellow and white and, here and there, groups of Bedouin tents.

After one more night in Petra we left for Aqaba, but with a stop to visit the last of the mines, Eshadiya. This is by far the largest, employing some one thousand men and also using draglines in the mining of the phosphate. There are vast storage silos and when I agreed to go to the top of one, it was in a wire cage attached to the side of the silo. Even the floor was wire mesh, and looking down to the ground as we rose some 400 feet was rather unnerving! The view from the top was spectacular, if you can call flat desert and a mining complex spectacular. But I did obtain some excellent pictures and it's not every day that one has such an experience.

Then on to Aqaba, where I had a superb room at the newly opened Intercontinental, with a view over the sea to the port. Next morning, we drove south along the corniche to the JPMC Fertiliser Complex. The huge drying drums thrummed, while steam expelled from the immensely tall, thin chimneys. Here sulphuric and phosphoric acid is produced and sold abroad. It was noisy and smelly and I was glad to leave and go to the dock area to meet the JPMC manager. Having come so far, I especially wanted to drive out to the actual phosphate jetty and go aboard a ship loading phosphate for India. This I did, and we boarded the ship by way of a very wobbly rope gangway slung alongside. As I moved along the deck to the holds, the captain called out to ask why I was there. My guide explained all and the captain then shouted down to me, 'OK, but only two pictures.' I shouted back, 'Yes!' Finally, after climbing a couple of iron rungs, I looked deep down into a hold already half filled with phosphate and took the two pictures. Now, from mines to ship, I had a complete record.

I was expecting to drive back to Amman but, with great kindness, the company arranged for me to take the evening flight to Amman where Saleh and Imad met me at the airport and drove me home. A first and most memorable and truly enjoyable trip in every way.

As soon as I was settled again I had all the films developed and, with some anxiety, awaited the results of more than two hundred exposures. After all, I was only using my manual Yashica cameras, one for distance and the other for close-ups, and I had no idea how the giant structures used at the mines would look. Thankfully, the vast majority turned out very well and the exceptionally clear, sunny weather greatly helped to enhance the pictures of draglines, silos, turbines and graders, not to mention the enormous stacks of drying phosphate.

Although I had not yet made any other 'official' trips for JPMC, I continued to be responsible for their ongoing stationery requirements and when Mr Kurdi's son, Sa'ad, joined the company in 2008, he asked for some large prints of Jordan to hang along the corridor walls of the company building. Sa'ad's mother, Princess Basma, had previously bought a number of my pictures and Sa'ad wanted some of the same, as well as others of the mines and also the newly opened Abdoun Suspension Bridge. From the road where I lived I could view the bridge perfectly, and one day stopped above it, close by a flowering Judas tree. It immediately struck me as an interesting subject and – snap! The picture records one of Amman's modern structures. Since then there has been a noticeable increase in state-of-the-art buildings, but nothing to compare with the bridge.

* * * * *

It is very sad to see so many private houses being demolished to make room for blocks of flats or business premises. Until the economic downturn forced much reconstruction either to slow down or stop, there was a crazy rush to get in on the building boom. As a result, uptown Amman has changed, in some places almost beyond recognition. In one area, small, traditional shops and businesses have long since been bought out and the entire street is now a row of jewellers' glass-fronted windows displaying glittering and costly rings, necklaces, brooches and other sparkling trinkets. It makes me think of London's Hatton Garden, home of just such expensive geegaws.

What concerns me more is the increasing loss of Jordanian 'essence' – that is, the flavour of local shops run by local people with close and friendly relations to their customers. I experience it in the same way with my Jordanian friends – always greetings, and often an enquiry about the family, followed perhaps by news of a daughter's engagement or the arrival of a grandson. So are friendships bonded and interests shared. I see these small enclaves of family businesses dwindling and replaced by poor quality, eye-catching knick-knack premises offering the endless glitzy array of accessories so dear to the young. These shops are almost cheek-by-jowl in some streets.

Even more disturbing to my mind is the construction of 'gated' complexes in rural areas. In one particular instance, about half an hour's run out of Amman, would-be luxury dwellings are rearing their concrete shapes among ancient oak trees. Whoever owns the land, to my mind it is being put to a display of costly comfort, most probably for foreign investors. It would seem that these communities are built to cater for moneyed people from abroad rather than the Jordanian citizen.

Down south in Aqaba, even the hotels are in sequestered areas, clustered together and sharing the limited beachfront which is inaccessible to the ordinary denizen, except with payment and always after personal inspection. Many of the same hotels also line the Dead Sea corniche and form a city like horizon, while the ever receding sea lies further out, and in between is a grey-brown mud flat.

Meanwhile, north of Amman still remains much less sophisticated and, in many ways, much nicer. With my friend Diane, I have spent strange nights in strange 'hotels'. Irbid, the largest city in that region and boasting a lively university, offers various hotels. However, we had yet to locate any such when on one of our northern excursions we stayed in a place marked 'hotel' – but consisting only of several bedrooms with the barest amenities. Our pad had two beds, a carpet thick with dust and grime, an unclean shower and that was it. But as usual, we managed and had a lot of laughter over it. Wearing thick socks, I leapt from floor to bed and had brought my own pillow case, in case! It was Ramadan and the inert lad working at reception, sleeping most of the time, had to stir himself to put on the geyser, and next morning provide breakfast.

As well as Irbid, we savoured Azraq and Umm Qais. The latter was a real test of endurance. It was December and, after a good drive along the Jordan Valley with frequent stops for photographs or fossil hunting, we arrived at the hilltop town of Umm Qais, one of the Roman cities of the Decapolis. We had booked in to the grandly named 'Umm Qais Hotel', but had no illusions. Offered a choice of two rooms, we opted for the slightly larger one; otherwise there was no difference. There were again two beds, one chair, a small table and a filthy shower. Leaving our packs there, we walked down the street to visit the considerable extent of Roman ruins. I like Umm Qais in that respect, and it is a place always enjoyed by local families who can wander along the lengthy street with its giant paving stones and many ruined houses either side. From its height you look straight across the hill slopes to Lake Tiberias.

We had a light meal at the site and returned to the hotel. The wind was rising and the temperature dropping, and bed was the best place. It was so cold that I dressed 'Pakistani' style – pyjamas, a shirt over them and a woollen jerkin on top. Get the picture? Diane took a photograph of me sitting on the edge of the bed and wearing my socks, too. Did we laugh! The wind howled all night, the storm rolled across the sky and the windows nearly left their frames. It was freezing. The only positive aspect was hot water for the shower. Next morning we had an illusory breakfast, packed up and left.

Our most recent exploit into local hospitality was at Azraq. No, not the more expensive RSCN Lodge, but a humbler Government Rest House along the road. It was some while since we had stayed there, and little was changed except that this time the large swimming pool was filled. The trees around it had grown, giving a greater sense of permanence and much needed shade during the summer months.

The layout of the two-bed adjoining chalets built around the pool and each with its own small patio is an excellent idea. Like so much in Jordan, proper and constant supervision would do wonders to such attractive places. Clean lavatories and basins, and provision of sufficient toilet paper should not be difficult to maintain. Likewise the restaurant service; it would be nice to have breakfast at neatly laid tables, and be offered such dishes as hummus, sliced goat's cheese, labneh, hardboiled eggs, zayt and za'atar and plenty of Arab bread.

Such is the gap between north and south, and I hope that the north will remain comparatively unspoilt. For me, there is a wealth of beauty and unknowns still to explore. The flora is particularly beautiful, due largely to the better climate. Then there are the dams. Yes, we do have quite a number, my most favourite being the King Talal Dam which, when full, reaches some 80 million cubic metres. It is strictly out of bounds to the general public but, because of my study and knowledge of the plants, I have permission at any time to go down there and drive along the road to the engineers' offices. These are sited on the little peninsula jutting out into the waters of the Zarka river which feeds the dam. No cars, no voices, no picnickers, just the gentle wind and birdsong.

13

The summer of 2007 took me back to the UK as always, and this time it included a lovely holiday in Dublin with some of my Irish cousins. I had never been to Dublin, and Veronica and David, who live just outside, are absolute experts on the city's history. Veronica is a much admired designer and weaver of Ireland's beautiful woollen cloth. It was bliss to have each excursion planned and Veronica as such an informed guide. Knowing my interest in history and ancient buildings, she took me to out-of-the-way places as well as art galleries, the university and cathedral and, to my great joy, I saw the Book of Kells. What exquisite paintings, calligraphy, colour, design.

She and I went up north into County Meath to look at the prehistoric Celtic site of Newgrange. Built in 3200 BC during the Neolithic period, therefore older than Stonehenge and the Egyptian pyramids, this monument is famous for the illumination of its passage and chamber by the winter solstice sun.

On another occasion, with David, we spent several hours at Powerscourt, a beautiful garden designed and laid out by Sir Edward Lutyens and Gertrude Jekyll. I hear it has been restored to its former glory since my visit and I would love to see it again. Veronica and I are very close in age, just one month apart, and we both have a deep interest in family history and genealogy, so part of the fun was just talking about our connections. David is an interesting person, too. He has written several books on the legends and history of Ireland and takes a keen interest in Veronica's ploys.

Back again in England, I stayed with my niece Christina, Harry and their young son Tom. Harry trains racehorses in Lambourn and has a full, flourishing yard. I went out early one morning with him to watch the horses exercising on the gallops. Time with Colin and Anne in Dorset was always so happy and relaxing, and I flew back to Amman much refreshed.

Christmas was held at my flat with ten of us seated round the dining room table – a very jolly affair with just one man, Alan Fellowes. He kindly agreed to be an honorary lady for the occasion. One friend had cooked a superb turkey, others the vegetables and special bits. I did puddings and everyone brought wine. So 2007 drew to a close.

14

By the spring of 2008 Diane and I had decided to take a trip to India and spent several months in preparation. We both wanted to be in the north, and I especially hoped to see Kashmir again. Thanks to a kind friend we were given the address of a tour operator in Delhi, going under the strange name of Incentive Destinations. They proved to be most helpful and so, between our ideas and their advice on certain points, we arranged a fifteen-day visit for the end of July. An overnight flight from Amman saw us arrive in Delhi the following morning where the Incentive Destinations agent met and took us to the Ferns Hotel. It was still very early, so after checking in we collapsed on our beds for a couple of hours' sleep. Do not think of a hotel situated off a tarmacked, tree-lined road. Rather, a fairly small three-storey building approached from a lane which opened up into an untidy space with a variety of trees and brilliant shrubs, and uneven ground. Clusters of children were running around an old rickshaw while their elders stared at us from their nearby shacks. Our room was adequate, clean and air-conditioned which we at once appreciated, the heat and humidity outside being high.

We received a phone call later that morning from a Mrs Harinda Matai. She is the office manager for a very big Indian company called Tradex. Her boss, Mr Gupta, was closely associated with the Jordan Phosphate Mines Company, and we had been given her name most kindly by Princess Basma. Known to everyone as Chuchu, Mrs Matai was marvellously kind, and such a charming lady with it. We both fell for her. She whisked us out to a waiting car and introduced us to her sister, another charmer called Rani. Knowing already some of our interests, she showed us round an unusual garden filled with exotic plants and statues, many of them representations of Hindu gods and goddesses.

Following a real Indian meal, all chosen by the ladies, we then drove along some of the main streets to view enormous Hindu and Sikh temples. Our next venue was the famous Red Fort, built of sandstone by the Moghul Emperor Shah Jahan, between 1638 and 1648. Since parking in or near the fort is prohibited, we left the car and took three rickshaws, riding line astern into the dense, swirling mass of shouting, honking cars, mopeds and rickshaws, clinging on for dear life to the sides of our vehicle as we wove in and out or suddenly shot across the road. But we made the fort and entered by the Lahore Gate, where so much fighting and heroism during the Mutiny is remembered.

For me, it was like walking in the past and yet not unfamiliar. I have loved history all my life and, in particular, military history. Here was the evidence of so much that I had read: the massive walls that ring the fort, and inside such a complete contrast. One is immediately struck by the immensity of the space within – there are green lawns edged with paths lined with flowers, and trees of great age give shade. Families were grouped here and there, children running freely, laughing and holding kites or enjoying a picnic. On the far side of this sward stands the beautiful Diwan-i-Khas. This was the Hall of Private Audiences in which the Emperor held meetings with courtiers and state guests. Opensided, its ceiling is a wonder of architecture and the pillars are faced with marble, on which flowers have been etched and painted. Close by is the Diwan-i-Aam. Also opensided, this was the Hall of Public Audiences where the Emperor heard complaints and pleas of the commoners. I took pictures of everything possible, and have turned some of them into cards to share my delight and pleasure with others not able to see for themselves these marvels of building design and beauty. Beyond the Diwans lies another lovely edifice, the Pearl Mosque, built entirely of marble by Aurangzeb, son of Shah Jahan. A man noted for his extreme cruelty, he was a devout Muslim. Strangely enough, his father had never built a mosque inside the fort, but instead erected the massive and magnificent Jama Masjid outside the walls, just a horse ride away. So Aurangzeb built his own. At one time the Jumna flowed below the battlements. A river was an essential element in Moghul building, but sadly the Jumna was later diverted and now there is only the ghostline of a wadi bed.

37. A train carrying phosphate through Wadi Rum to the port of Aqaba

38. Anchored cargo vessels lying offshore near Aqaba port

39. Bedouin tent in the hills above the Jordan Valley

40. Weathered sandstone rock in the desert of Wadi Rum, Jordan

41. Prayer flags fluttering above the 13,700 ft. Fotula Pass, Ladakh 2008

42. Tibetan children at the SOS village in Choglamsar, Ladakh 2008

43. Decorating papier mâché boxes, Srinagar, Kashmir 2008

44. Using an acetylene lamp to remove fluff from a newly finished Kashmir rug, Srinagar 2008

45. Colourful bazaar scene in Srinagar, Kashmir 2008

46. The Shah Hamdan Mosque, rebuilt in the eighteenth century after several fires, standing beside the Jhelum River, Srinagar

47. Attractively decorated traditional brick-built houses in Srinagar

48. Wearing lotus-leaf hats, lads fish in the rain on Lake Nagin. Srinagar 2008

49. A floating general store on Lake Nagin

50. Damaged tower of the
once beautiful St. Paul's
Church, Ambala 2009

HISTORY OF ST PAUL'S CHURCH

ST PAUL'S CHURCH WAS CONSECRATED ON 04 JAN 1857 BY THE
AUTHORITY OF LORD BISHOP DANIEL OF CALCUTTA AND BISHOP DEALTRY OF
MADRAS. THE CHURCH WAS BUILT IN DECORATED GOTHIC STYLE AND HAD A
SEATING CAPACITY FOR 1500 PEOPLE. IT WAS A GARRISON CHURCH,
SPECIALLY MEANT FOR BRITISH ARMY OFFICERS, MEN AND THIER FAMILIES
THOUGH CIVILIANS ALSO JOINED IN THE WORSHIP. THE CHURCH WAS
INITIALLY AFFILIATED TO THE CHURCH OF ENGLAND BUT ON 03 APR 1925,
IT WAS SHIFTED TO LAHORE DIOCESE. IT IS BELIEVED THAT THIS IS THE
OLDEST CHURCH IN THE STATE OF HARYANA.

ON 21 SEP 1965, DURING THE INDO-PAK CONFLICT, ST PAUL'S
CHURCH WAS DESTROYED DUE TO INDISCRIMINATE BOMBING BY
PAKISTAN'S AIR FORCE. LEADERS FROM ALL OVER THE WORLD CONDEMNED
THIS INCIDENT AND TERMED IT AS A CRIME AGAINST HUMANITY.

51. Board describing the
church's history, Ambala

52. Passing this elephant, I stopped the car and raced back to take a picture. Delhi 2009

53. At 239 ft, the twelfth-century Qutab Minar is the tallest existing brick minaret. Delhi 2009

54. The Red Fort in Delhi, built of sandstone by the Moghul Emperor, Shah Jehan, between 1638-48

What a first day! The next two days were spent partly in … guess where? Bookshops! They sound strange places to be but the choice of books and the immense amount of reading Indians enjoy is amazing. Coming from Jordan with its rather restricted choice, it was marvellous to have the leisure to browse and just look at the width and variety of reading material. Prices are much more competitive than here in Amman, and both Diane and I left with a considerable number of books.

Chuchu was quite indefatigable, sparing endless time taking us wherever we wanted and then to look at shoes and clothes and jewellery. There was such a choice and much of it so affordable too. We looked at the National Gallery and a folk museum, and one other remarkable edifice, the Qutb Minar. This brick tower, built in 1193, is of Indo-Islamic architecture and, at a height of 234 feet, is the only one of its kind now in existence. Within the same complex stands the Jain temple and Hall of Pillars, each one intricately carved.

Early the following morning, we left on a flight to Leh, the capital of Ladakh. This extreme northern region of India was once an independent kingdom. Leh itself is bounded by the Himalayas and Karakoram, and transversely between the Ladakh and Zaskar ranges. It lies in a rain shadow often known as the high altitude cold desert of northern India. The plane was small and our luggage weight had to be halved. We were going to fly high to get over the mountains, and in the thin air the aircraft needed to be as light as possible. We arrived in Leh and descended to the tarmac at an altitude of 11,500 feet, literally catching our breath – at least I was. We were met by our travel agent and taken to the pleasant hotel amidst its flowery garden, with views of the snowcapped mountains beyond. Feeling suddenly tired and sleepy, we dossed down until the afternoon in order to acclimatize in preparation for the rest of our stay in Ladakh.

Later we met our fine team with the four-wheel drive. Both young Ladakhis, Stenbah the driver and Nurbo the guide, were very friendly and we got on famously from the first. We also made it clear that we were not necessarily going to stick to the itinerary but rather, if there was something of added interest en route to our planned destination then we would go and see it. The lads were very easy on this and rather enjoyed doing something different. They knew the country backwards and many times we stopped for me to take pictures of flowers, or the Indus on its great journey, or unusual scenery. That was the joy of planning just for ourselves.

We visited many different monasteries; Ladakh being essentially a Buddhist region, there are dozens and dozens. They are often built high up at the end of deep and barely accessible valleys. Life is very spartan and rigorous with absolutely no frills. The monks spend many hours at prayer, as well as teaching the young novices and working whatever land is available – a lifetime of discipline and obedience. Buddhism is a way of life, and most families with sons will automatically send one or more to live the monastic way.

There is no easy approach to a monastery building and I was often daunted when I looked at the countless steps climbing upwards. Diane, who is considerably younger than me, sped on with the guide and I was left to make my own way up. I am pleased to say that I always made it – in the end! The views were spectacular, and many of the monasteries housed beautiful artefacts. While walking around one of the oldest monasteries, Lamayuru, I suddenly heard a familiar sound and, turning round, saw two elderly nuns, each with a bell. As they came closer, I heard them intoning words that my father had told us about all those years ago when he served in Tibet: 'Um mane padme hum', 'O, the jewel in the lotus'. I never forgot them and know that it is like reading beads. This vast monastery is the last one before crossing the border from Ladakh into Kashmir. Its members belong to the Red Hat Order and number some one hundred monks in residence. There is also a large religious college attached and a sizeable library. A guest house provides basic accommodation, particularly for pilgrims and backpackers on mountain treks during the summer months.

One morning, we drove south a short distance out of Leh to the SOS village of Choglamsar. Here, close to the Indus, a school has been established for refugee Tibetan boys and girls. The majority live in, the younger children housed in rooms built around a courtyard. With two or four to a room with bunk beds, each child has their own private space for books or photographs, or even a toy or two.

We did not have time to see the older students, but spent a while in a large, light classroom among the young ones. All seated on the carpeted floor in different groups, amazed to see us, they stared with huge brown eyes at these odd-looking, white-skinned strangers. Di and I moved amongst them getting down to look at their books or games and, sometimes stretched full length on the floor, I was able to catch shots of shy, smiling little faces. The teacher, also seated on the floor, had a low table where any child could come for help – and sometimes a gentle chastisement. Picture some thirty under-fives, many of them so lively and so naughty, but so charming with it.

Leaving the village, we broke away from any fixed plans that day and went wherever Stenbah or Nurbo suggested. This included several unscheduled stops and, for me, determination to get some good pictures of the Indus. This mighty waterway, still in its infancy here, has a total length of 3,180 kilometres (1,980 miles) before it exits into the Arabian Sea near Karachi. I have a favourite photo of the river running below a small and lonely monastery perched high up on a rocky prominence above the water.

The food at the hotel was excellent and I rather over indulged. Buddhists are vegetarians and, although we had no meat, the dishes all looked and proved to be so inviting. There was a wonderful variety of vegetables, some of which were quite new to us, as well as pulses and, of course, rice, all accompanied by delicious homemade breads.

Shy young girls cleaned our room and took our laundry, often giggling the while, as we tried to make ourselves understood. We left any shopping until the end of our stay in Leh and much enjoyed exploring the back streets of the mountain town. Few roads are tarmacked, just hard-packed earth, and with little or no street lighting it was easy to get lost.

I bought a locally made rug and later a Kashmiri *numdah* (an embroidered North Indian rug woven from coarse felt), both of which adorn my home. Kashmir exports a lot of goods to Leh and it was quite hard to find the genuine local products. Remember that there is only one road between Srinagar and Leh and after mid October, snow closes it completely until the end of April.

Very early on 6th August we left Leh with many happy and entertaining thoughts, to begin the nearly 500 mile, two-night stop to Srinagar. The road that I mentioned earlier was, to start with, a properly surfaced highway, if bending and narrow from time to time. We soon left habitation behind, driving for long spells with no sign of dwellings. What became more and more interesting and exciting was the violent change of scenery. The mountains began to appear from nowhere, keeping the road hemmed in on either side. Sheer grey rocks towered above us and fell away for hundreds of feet below. At the bottom of the precipice ran the ever flowing rivers; we stopped to get out and look at the confluence of the Indus and the Zanskar joining forces as the River Indus, to run its two thousand-mile course to the sea. This is another of my favourite pictures and was the start of a photographic dream.

Later we turned off the road to take a track winding into a high valley and visit what, for me, was one of the most interesting and attractive of the monasteries – Basgo. It is listed as an endangered site by the World Monument Fund. Built of mud and brick during the sixteenth and seventeenth centuries, the fortress has three temples.

Throughout my stay in Ladakh, I was struck by the austere conditions in which not only the monks lived, but also the ordinary town or village dwellers. It is a very harsh land and demands a stalwart, hardy and resilient people to survive the bitter cold of winter.

As the snows slowly melt, they feed the endless mountain streams which gather force and flow swiftly down to the broad flat valleys, some of which are several kilometres across. Willows and poplars often line these waterways and are grown in great numbers; there is hardly another species of tree produced. This is because both are absolutely essential in house building; the trunks of the poplars form the framework with infilling of dried mud and straw, and the willows are woven to be laid as a basis for thatch. The overall view is one of green and grey, fields awash with a mixture of vegetables and maize, and all around them stand the slate coloured mountains, the slopes razor-edged and the tops sharp as needles. With only five months for sowing and harvesting, every bit of soil is cultivated.

Before beginning the mountain climb, we passed through several villages, frequently stopping at the outskirts and walking through. With so many interesting things to look at (we were always objects of attention too), we poked our noses into the small shops, sniffing herbs and asking what was this and that. On the sidewalk women were selling small baskets of apricots. This is a very popular fruit throughout Ladakh and is generally dried for use during the winter months. The flat rooftops would often have fruit out to dry and, on one occasion, I noted that hay was piled along the roof edges for later use as animal fodder. Houses, at most three storeys, with open verandahs and a wonderful array of plants such as vines, pots of marigolds, geraniums and cannas, were always bedecked with flags.

In time we came to Alchi, the only *gompa* in the Ladakh region built on level ground. The monastery was founded in the eleventh century and is noted for its massive Buddha statues. There are other statues made of clay and, unusually, also lavishly painted wood carvings from Kashmir.

From there it was a short run on to Ole Tokpo, our first night's stop. Reading about it when planning our trip, we were not very impressed with the thought of camping in tents. On entering the complex, however, we found something rather different. It is situated amidst olive trees with a pretty flower garden planted around a lawn. The 'tent' aspect was that of a tent, but with wooden walls, two small windows and a canvas roof. Inside were a couple of simple beds, a few clothes hooks and a small table with a naked light bulb.

The complex was of fairly recent construction and aimed chiefly at serious long-distance mountain walkers. In a region otherwise devoid of creature comforts, Ole Tokpo was the perfect stopover. It had excellent laundry facilities and unusual washing arrangements, as we soon discovered. To shower or go to the loo, you had to walk over to a building with a line of outside wash basins, or take a shower in one of the cabins. The water was wonderfully hot. So, in the morning you might be doing your teeth, standing beside someone shaving. Night time was a bit trickier but, thanks to Diane's torch, I was able to navigate myself to the lavatory in my pyjamas and slippers.

The restaurant was a proper building, and here we served ourselves and ate at long tables. Again the food was vegetarian, but beer was available for those wishing for a stronger brew. I wandered all round the compound and then unexpectedly came to a thatched shelter and, on going to look over the edge, saw the dear old Indus rushing along, grey and muddy, way below. On the far bank there was a serious attempt at terracing and rows of plants were growing. I couldn't be sure what they were, probably vegetables.

Early next day we began the most dramatic and exciting part of our journey, the road beginning to break up and the mountains rising ever higher. I became intoxicated with their shape, their colour, their immensity and sheer grandeur. Their beauty was enhanced by the grey and white cloud formations scudding high above, across a brilliant blue sky. The valleys lying so deep and so far below seemed devoid of life, but occasionally I glimpsed a pencil-thin watercourse and small patches of vivid green.

* * * * *

We were now travelling entirely surrounded by mountains, up and up until we suddenly came across a large yellow sign. On it was written in English, 'Fotula Pass 13,749 ft'. We had reached the highest point of our journey. Of course, we stopped to get out and look around. On one side, I saw the ground falling steeply away and, in the distance, a very strangely shaped rock protruding from the top of a mountain. Immediately in front of me was a rough post and, attached all along a rope, were coloured prayer flags whirling crazily in the violent wind. It was an irresistible picture and hangs in my sitting room today.

So, having recorded something on one side, I moved over to look at the other valley. An entirely different picture met my eye and, in my excitement, I nearly missed getting a shot. Here, the valley was climbing more gently up to the pass, shallow and filled with loose grey shale. In a slow-moving line was a donkey train. The beasts were loose and making their own way, some with young ones, and a number being ridden as pack animals. I learnt that these people make the trip

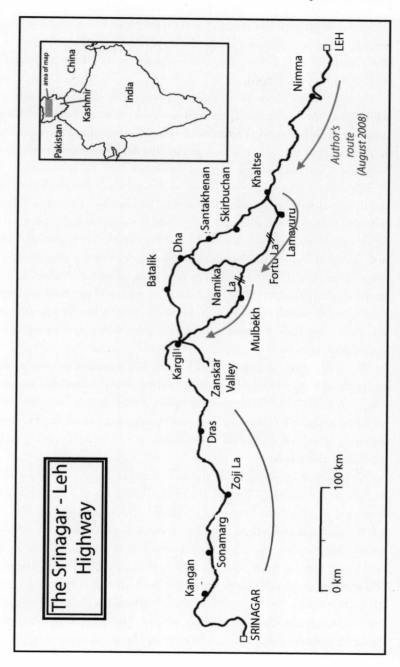

down to the plain in late spring, taking their goods to sell and stocking up on the necessities for a long winter, before beginning the two to three months' trek home. The thrill and drama of that time lingers with me still.

Coming slowly out from the high ranges we descended into a valley.Here the barley had been harvested and was standing in stooks – another lovely scene to be recorded. The road ran along the river for some time and we stopped for a picnic, overlooking green fields and large vegetable plots all set amongst willows.

The next night-stop was to be at Kargil and the road turned northwest as we again climbed, crossing the Namkila Pass, and drove through Drass, which is noted for its heavy snowfalls and reputed to be the second-coldest inhabited place in the world. It was getting dark and the road had virtually ceased to exist, now simply a dust covered track littered with rocks and large boulders, all of which had to be negotiated, bearing in mind the decreasing width of the road and the sheer drop of hundreds of feet. It was quite hair-raising in places, but our driver, Stenbah, knew exactly what he was doing and we had full confidence in him.

We finally reached Kargil. This is a military base and was the scene of much fighting during the Indian/Pakistan border conflict between May and July 1999. Visitors travelling between Leh and Srinagar have to make a night halt here before continuing the second leg of their journey. It is not to be recommended, a very dirty, scruffy and extremely noisy town.

We were put up in probably the only possible 'hotel', which I write in inverted commas. Written above the Urdu hotel sign were the facetious words, 'Your Home from Home'. To start with, we had to ask for blankets and a light. The bathroom was grim and the washing system Methuselan; there was even a urinal on one wall. Of course Di and I both saw the funny side of all these things and had a good laugh. We entered the dining room to find it packed with a large group of very disgruntled French tourists, and eventually squeezed ourselves onto a bench seating some twenty others. The waiters raced about bringing plates of food, some meat stew and far from appetizing; there was no other choice. This was followed by an apple and a banana. Di, who likes her drink, managed to get a waiter to smuggle a bottle of beer, slightly disguised. Considering we were in Pakistan, it was a brave act! There was absolutely nothing to do and certainly no going into the town or even taking a walk, so we went to bed and read.

Because of the fear of attacks on single vehicles travelling close to the border, our driver, Stenbah, had arranged for us to join a small convoy of four-wheel drives for the final lap to Srinagar. We were to leave at 0200 hours. So, alarms set, we duly awoke and were ready at the appointed hour, only to discover that the convoy had left without us. There was nothing for it but to set off immediately in the hope that we might catch up with them. I don't know how Stenbah, in the pitch black, was able to navigate the narrow road, densely lined with trees and always with the threat of that sheer drop. We never saw the convoy. Eventually we reached the border, not that you would ever have guessed it: a small hut with a single light and not even on the road, but across rough ground amidst some broken down shacks. Di and I got out to stretch our legs, but didn't venture more than a few yards for fear of stumbling over bits of iron or barbed wire. Anyway, our passports were duly stamped and we pressed on.

By now we were starting to descend, but progress was very slow as the road continued to deteriorate. From time to time we met a lorry, vastly overladen and simply crawling around the boulders. It would be another three days before the driver reached Leh. As the mountains receded we began to enter the treeline, thousands of conifers above us on the high hills. It was a relief to see signs of life, and soon other trees came into view, in particular the cedar (chenar) from which so much of the famous Kashmiri carved woodwork is produced.

At last, we entered the summer resort of Sonamarg. It was only 0500 hours, but we found a small café and were served sweet tea by the Sikh owner before the last lap to Srinagar. Our road ran alongside a sparkling, cascading river and, joy, there were numerous wild flowers growing on the banks, none of which I could identify. An hour later we entered the environs of Srinagar. It was Friday and, with the unsettled political situation, we didn't want to be driving into throngs of people heading for mosque prayers. We reached our rendezvous and awaited the houseboat owner. Naba Wagnoo, a small, bearded man, dressed entirely in white, a hadji cap on his head, stepped out of his vehicle and we shook hands. We thanked Stenbah and Nurbo who had brought us safely the whole way, wished them a good return and handed each a generous tip. Then into Naba's four-wheel with his driver, to take us out to Lake Nagin and our waiting houseboat, the Lady Juliette.

Kashmir! A word to evoke so many memories. Poetry, painting, passion and, sadly, Partition. I had last seen these mountains and lakes and wooden houses as a twelve-year-old girl, making the daily crossing of the Jhelum River on my way to school in Srinagar. Now it was to cross a small bridge and enter a houseboat. Karim the bearer welcomed us aboard and, taking the baggage, led us along a narrow passage, first to the bedroom. With diamond window panes, curtains and matching bedspreads, carpeted wooden floors, it was to be our resting place for the next five nights. At the other end of the boat we entered a dining room and through it into a large sitting room before coming out onto the balcony – not just any old balcony, but one with cushioned seats arranged around three sides of the carved wooden balustrade, and a small gate opening to steps leading down to the water. The views ... but you must wait awhile.

The most striking feature throughout the entire boat was the decoration. The ceilings, the walls, the window frames were beautifully carved in cedar wood. The panels dividing the sitting and dining rooms depicted birds, lotus flowers and the leaf of the cedar tree, and were backed by a dark turquoise-blue glass. The walls continued with a similar motif, but without the glass, and the ceiling was of a large honeycomb design. Lovely curtains hung at the windows, all made from a heavy cream-coloured cotton and embroidered with birds and flowers. A red carpet covered the floors. We were in the land of the Moghuls.

Much time was spent on the balcony, and I often rose early to try and catch that special picture. The lake was empty of boats at such an hour, except for a lone fisherman who came regularly to cast his line into the cool, still water. Behind him were the mountains and a gentle sun, but the mist lingered over the water, hiding everything, adding mystery and a subtle colour to the scene. Later the lake became alive with movement. Vendors paddled from houseboat to houseboat calling out their wares, and were often very persistent in trying to get you to buy. They were not allowed onto a boat without permission, so had to work hard displaying papier mâché boxes, scarves, silver jewellery or fancily stitched leather slippers and small wood carvings amongst their many souvenirs.

The Lady Juliette was one of a number of boats tied up at the edge of the lake, and we watched with interest the arrival of the vegetable man each day. He travelled up and down the lake selling his produce and, according to our choice, he brought not only vegetables familiar to us but also a variety of others we had never seen. Karim told us something about them, and we asked to try a new one for dinner each night, eating them as accompaniments to our delicious Kashmiri curry. Sadly, I cannot recall their names now, except one. This is the cock's comb (Celonia argenta), an extraordinary plant, its brilliant red, orange or yellow floral structure composed of a series of deeply waved sections. It is dried and sold in many of the spice shops..

Lake Nagin is a few kilometres out of Srinagar and we enjoyed ourselves immensely just relaxing on our 'quarter deck', experimenting with our new cameras and often spending several hours travelling across the lake with Farouk, the pleasant shikara wallah (boatman). Shikaras are similar in some ways to gondolas, but lightly built and propelled with a single flat oar. Parts of the lake are covered with lotus (Nelumbo nucifera). Their flowers are exquisite, the petalled blooms, shades of pink. The lotus is the national flower of Kashmir and every part of it – from root to seed – is of use, either as a foodstuff or medicinally. The seed pods, which look like giant poppy heads, are very tasty both green or dried, and sometimes roasted. We often met women, their shikaras loaded with the stems and leaves, paddling home, taking the fodder for their animals, particularly cows.

Farouk took us up little weed covered passages to see some of the villages set only just above the water. On tiny plots of land, really false islands made from accumulated mud and dead greenery, they grew vegetables. One, which we ate one evening, was hanging from a vine-like stem and looked like an elongated courgette. Other plots had lovely gardens ablaze with zinnias and the dark purple love-lies-bleeding. Gliding over the water, seeing something different at almost every turn, one was in another world. It was hard to imagine that this beautiful country we were so enjoying continued to be rift apart with violence, hatred and death.

* * * * *

One of the places I had set my heart on seeing again was Gulmarg. It was not to be. With serious street fighting and blockades in and around Srinagar, it was impossible to take that road. I found myself thinking back to those halcyon days of 1943 in Gulmarg with nostalgia, where my mother, Colin and I had spent almost one year. We were privileged to live in such beautiful and peaceful surroundings, far from the horrors of war. Many times we walked along one of the circular roads from where we could see the grandeur of the snow-clad mountains of the Himalayas. The brilliant sparkle of sunshine and contrast of purple shadows falling on each peak was an unforgettable picture. Nanga Parbat (The Bare Maiden) could be clearly seen, rising over 24,000 feet, along with a glory of other mountains.

* * * * *

Naba, who was looking after us so well, took us instead to the Lidda River, which he knew I also wanted to see again. In 1943 my father had spent a brief leave with us and, as a keen fisherman, had decided to camp by the Lidda river, not far from Pahalgam. Together we spent a happy few days, Pa angling for trout and Colin catching his first fish, some five inches long and cooked for breakfast later. So, once again, I saw the wide, fast-flowing river and here, with Di, Naba and our driver, we had our picnic.

One day, Naba, a devout Muslim, was going into Srinagar to pray at the Shah Hamdan mosque, and we insisted on accompanying him to town. The Shah Hamdan is an interesting and ancient building.

Situated beside the Jhelum River which flows through the city, the mosque is built mostly of wood. After being burned down and rebuilt several times, it was restored in the seventeenth century by Aurangzeb, son of Shah Jahan.

Since no foreign women are permitted entry to the mosque, Naba suggested we go round the corner and look at some ancient murals. We found the wall and I stared at it in amazement. From top to bottom, it was covered in beautiful floral designs. Entirely Islamic, they had been painted on the papier mâché wall-facing several hundred years earlier. The designs were Persian, and all the more remarkable for their superb condition. Exposed to wind, rain, sun and snow all those years, they still retained their vibrant colour. I learnt later that the dyes used were derived from minerals rather than those of plants.

With Naba still at prayer, we then ventured into the town and wandered around, not bothered or molested, only asked occasional questions in English. We were a rare sight, especially two women walking alone. When Naba emerged from the mosque and did not see us, he got into a bit of a tizz. Luckily Di had her mobile and we soon made contact.

On another day out of town, we looked at some very old Hindu temples, then spent about an hour in a cricket bat workshop. Di had spied the bats hanging outside and we nipped across the road to inspect, leaving our host and driver in the car. We penetrated behind huge piles of bats awaiting manufacture and, amongst the trees, came to a small sawmill. Four young men enthusiastically showed us round, speaking excellent English. We saw the creation of a bat from start to finish, and were proudly informed that these products were considered some of the very highest standard and bought by famous batsmen.

Throughout our trip, we had been fortunate with the weather by and large, but one day whilst out on the lake with Farouk, it began to rain. We were under cover but Farouk was not, and Di tossed him her mackintosh. He took us to another part of the lake and here we saw some youths fishing. Viewing them from the rear was really funny. Picture a shikara with several backs all a little bent as they held their rods, and on top of each head an enormous lotus leaf – another use.

On our return to the houseboat, as it was the last day, we thanked Farouk and gave him a generous tip. He had removed the mac but did not offer to return it. That was not bad manners, just the custom.

There were so many memorable occasions. Yet another was a visit to the famed Shalimar Gardens which lie close to the Dal Lake. Again with Naba, we strolled around this lovely place set amidst trees, canals and waterfalls with the forested mountains a backdrop. The gardens were created in 1619 by the emperor Jahangir for his wife, Nur Jahan.

Last, but not least, was the opportunity to see the weaving, washing and finishing of a Kashmiri carpet, the hand painting on papier mâché boxes, and finally to visit the Naba family showroom. Here we revelled in the fantastic display of rugs, silk scarves, pashminas that run through a ring, embroidered bedspreads and exquisitely stitched jackets. I managed to curb my spending inclinations, and bought two bedspreads and a beautiful, long, black evening jacket made of the finest of fine wool. One of the bedspreads graces my bed all summer long.

Srinagar is a combination of two Sanskrit words: sri means wealth and abundance, and nagar means a city. Despite the bombardment and destruction of parts of the city, we were able to find, even amongst the poverty-ridden streets and back alleys, beautiful old wooden houses with their fretwork balconies and turquoise-painted door and window frames. Other houses were built of warm pinkish brick, having attractive brick designs inset around the tops of windows in a semi-circular form. I found friendliness and kindly service in shops and with all the people I met. May I return once more.

On arrival back in Delhi, we were taken to visit Mr and Mrs Gupta. Ajay Gupta is the Managing Director of Tradex where our good friend Chuchu works. Here Di and I were each presented with beautiful embroidered stoles and superb books on India in which Ajay kindly inscribed. We had gone to them unchanged, really scruffy from our recent travels, and I was quite embarrassed to be sitting in their elegant drawing room with my dusty trainers and creased jeans.

The following day we travelled back to Amman and had the pleasure of looking at the lovely gifts and assembling the memories of a remarkable journey.

15

As soon as I was settled, I sent the family a long email detailing all our exploits and was delighted at their response. Colin found it most interesting and Johnny was equally enthralled. I was really chuffed since both brother and nephew are writers of some skill. I kept a copy for myself and am glad I did so, as it is too easy to forget many little incidents (although one always swears it will never be the case).

The months slipped by into Christmas, with its charity bazaars and my work producing another calendar for the Phosphate Company. All through the autumn I had felt that I had not really rounded off my trip to India. There was still the much hoped for visit to Agra and a longing to go north to Ambala once more. My dear friend, Chuchu, knew this and encouraged me in every way to come back again soon. I pondered long, wondering if I was just being self-indulgent or, in common sense terms, could I afford it? I then wrote to dear Colin for his sound advice, and he simply replied, 'Go for it.' So on 25th January, the day that would have been John's and my forty-fifth wedding anniversary, I flew to Delhi once again.

Chuchu had kindly booked me into a B&B close to their house in south Delhi, and I was met at the airport by a driver and taken to my lodging early the next morning. How good it was to feel the warmth, see greenery and flowers, and smell the damp earth. In my bedroom I found a choice of teas, biscuits and fruit as well as a lovely flower arrangement, all from Chuchu. To add further to my convenience, Mr Gupta had arranged for me to have the daily use of a Landrover together with a Nepalese driver called Govind. This way I was quite independent, yet had the luxury of full-time transport. Just as well, since getting anywhere in Delhi is a nightmare, cars, buses, rickshaws and the three-wheeled tuk-tuks all vying for space on the overcrowded thoroughfares. The places I wanted to visit were, on average, at least three-quarters of an hour from my pension.

I had to revisit the Red Fort, this time at my own pace, looking for other architectural gems I had not seen before. Marble pillars inlaid with floral designs, exquisite tracery on the carved domes and arches – just the size and proportion was overwhelming. 'Think big' must surely have been a permanent motto.

Once again I enjoyed looking at the pure white marble of the Moti Mahal or Pearl Mosque, built by Aurangzeb, the son of Shah Jahan. Strangely enough, there had not been a mosque within the precincts of the fort, Shah Jahan preferring to build the mighty Jama Masjid a short distance outside the walls. Aurangzeb, a strong believer, wanted his own place of prayer nearby.

One morning, in complete contrast Rani drove me to the Lodhi Gardens and let me loose for the next three hours while she sat and read. This was a first visit for me and I revelled in the space. Magnificent and varied trees grew throughout the area, most of them labelled which reminded me of Kew. The gardens are named after the Lodhi dynasty, which flourished alongside the Moghuls in the mid-sixteenth century. Several very fine family tombs are dotted around, similar in style, but differing considerably in decoration with lovely detailed doors and ceilings, and I had all the time to choose my shots.

Another first and memorable visit was to Humayun's tomb. He was considered to be Barbur's favourite son and succeeded him. This, to my mind, is one of the finest sites in Delhi. The grounds are vast and seem laid out to invite the visitor to enjoy all the lesser mausoleums and other attractive areas long before reaching Humayun's tomb itself. I found such an atmosphere of tranquility in all my wanderings. The tomb is magnificent, constructed of pink sandstone with beautiful detail on the massive doors, ceilings and certain walls, mostly in a fine Qur'anic script. I climbed steep steps to the large octagonal roof which in turn supports the dome, and looked in at the tomb itself – simple marble. Lovely views all around, green lawns and tall, slender, grey-trunked palms added majesty to the place. So much Moghul art, culture and architecture was influenced by Humayun's enforced exile in Persia, when his kingdom was occupied for several years by the most powerful of the Afghan leaders, Sher Shah Suri, before Humayun could regain it.

One day, I was exploring some alleyways and narrow streets lined with small 'antique' shops, when I suddenly came out onto a grassy space where a family group was enjoying a meal. Behind them stood an attractive mosque. Looking around with increasing curiosity, I spied extensive ruins and down below, a lake. So after a hasty lunch with Rani I retraced my steps for further exploration and plunged into the vast Baluchi Gardens Park. So very, very different from the Lodhi Gardens; only on a much grander scale, but wilder and unkempt. That to me only added to its attraction, together with the lake I had viewed earlier. Late afternoon light was falling on the lake, and I loved looking at the many skeletal trees, half drowned, but so perfectly reflected in the water. I think I have quite an addiction for reflections since very recently I photographed an apple orchard in north Jordan which each winter is flooded for weeks, and still the trees grow and bear fruit.

My pension was owned by a young Rajasthani divorcee who had some four to five rooms available. The two house boys who virtually looked after the place knew very little English, so I sometimes went into the kitchen to demonstrate how to make 'unda rumble tumble' (scrambled eggs) for other enquiring guests.

Once outside the gate it was absolutely 'India'. The roadway of hard-packed earth was lined with many fine private houses and varied trees; brilliant-hued bougainvillea scrambled up fences and in amongst the leaves came birdsong sweet and harsh, or the occasional monotonous call of the brainfever bird. The air was always pungent – be it dust or dung or jasmine, a mingling of ineradicable scents. It was so familiar, an integral part of my youth. Along this 'highway' one met everybody and everything. Strolling leisurely, I encountered old and young, man and beast: scrawny moth-eaten dogs dreaming in the sun or scratching their fleas but, strangely enough, not aggressive; elderly – or perhaps not so elderly – small, bent women with tired, lined eyes, and an impoverished mien, yet colourful in their vivid-hued saris.

I stopped to watch men playing drafts. Squatted on the ground, they were sipping tea or chewing betel nut in between their moves. There was generally an interested cluster of small boys throwing in their own comments. It wouldn't be that long before they, too, would be squatting on the ground! Postcard sellers, sweet sellers, beggars and incessant music provided a constant accompaniment. Tiny, often shack like Hindu shrines leant against crumbling walls, and all I could see or hear was a dark, flag-bedecked doorway, bells a'tinkling and the hum of prayer.

Small shops clustered along the main road, all untidy, their owners cheerful and chatty. Few foreigners ever seemed to be around and I was constantly invited in to view the wares. I didn't need anything, so called a thank you, but 'Don't want' in Urdu, which brought forth a torrent of friendly exclamations before I sped off. Although the layout of streets is fairly straightforward, being on a grid system, it was easy to take a wrong turn with such similarity between the dusty lanes. I had to memorize certain landmarks in order not to get too lost, or too tired.

My time was slipping by fast, but there were still two major visits to make. Early one morning saw Chuchu and me with Govind at the wheel, leaving Delhi's sprawl and heading north to Ambala. I was eager to see everything en route and, with the mist still clinging to the fields, there was a sort of secrecy about the landscape. Being so early, it was fun to glimpse women often squatting by small rivulets or even puddles with their dhobi (washing), or bullocks moving ponderously along dirt tracks, their carts laden with fodder or manure. These are indelible sights through all India and speak of tradition and permanence.

The towns seemed to merge one into another in a long straggling line broken by large swathes of mixed agriculture – some padi, vegetables and young corn. Thinking back, it seemed little had changed in the rural areas, although I was told most earning families would have a washing machine and certainly a television. There were bicycles everywhere, generally with two aboard, the lads so dexterous at skimming past vehicles or dodging between monstrous horn-blaring trucks. One could describe the road traffic as being in a state of permanent chaos, yet, with all the carts, loose animals, rickshaws and buses seemingly criss-crossing each other, I never actually saw an accident.

We stopped for a local breakfast and I found very nice T-shirts inscribed with 'Punjab' on the front and, on the reverse, some of the major towns in the region. I was reminded, however, that we were not in fact in Punjab, but in the state Haryana.

We entered Ambala by afternoon and first found the Sirhind Club. This fine building, as I had known it as a child, was essentially for adults only. With its superb lawns, year round flowerbeds and excellent tennis courts, it had been the hub of regimental sport, relaxation and entertainment. Of course there were certain times when all the family gathered for the wonderful children's parties or Christmas carols. At one such party I had received a Kodak Box Brownie. Extremely simple to use, with a remarkably good lens, it remained with me as my only camera until I was in my mid-twenties and still taking black and white pictures all through my teaching years in Malaya. Now there was not a soul in sight as we walked round to the back, across the bare, unkempt ground and knocked at the secretary's office. The official had only been there for fifteen years and told me that no records were kept after Partition in 1947; I got the feeling that they had been destroyed. So I asked about the gardens, tennis and squash courts. Everything had gone; there had been no attempt at upkeep except for some palm trees at the front.

I went inside and looked at the names of presidents, all Indians. Gone too, were the trophies, heads and silver. We met a young woman who showed us the ballroom with its stage. She told us that the building had been restored and painted but had received little structural alteration, and this I could immediately see from the ceiling and the old fans. It was almost eerie to think back to the time when Colin and I had been enlisted to take part in a ghastly play called Dr Sunder the Surgeon, forcefully masterminded and produced by the brigadier's wife, Mrs Bunbury. I would much like to have spoken to someone in authority and was saddened to see the once famous club so degenerated.

At St Paul's Anglican Church we located the Indian pastor, Reverend Bhatty, living in part of the one time rectory with his wife and grown children; the other part is now the church serving some forty local families. He walked with us across the rough field to the church, and I took good pictures at all angles to show the extensive damage that had been done to the building. There was some well displayed information about it and a brief history, all of which I recorded. One of the finest churches in British India, St Paul's was consecrated in January 1857 – the year of the Mutiny. In September 1965, during one of the several small wars between India and Pakistan, it was reported that, aiming to strike at the Indian airbase, the Pakistan Air Force had missed its target and instead hit the church. During all the different periods we had lived in Ambala we had attended Sunday morning service at St Paul's. Colin was born in September 1931 and I guessed he would have been christened there before the end of that year. I asked Reverend Bhatty if he had the registers going back that far and could look up Colin's name. I would be returning two days later to call in and see whether he had had any luck.

My final destination was to cross up and over the railway bridge which was exactly as I remembered it, and down into the Allenby Lines cantonment, our one time home, and headquarters of the 1/XV Training Battalion. I was so hoping to find the road and red-brick bungalow with its wide verandah, large shady trees and big garden. Alas, time would not permit a search up and down each road. Instead I took a picture or two of sadly neglected whitewashed bungalows, their gardens totally derelict, with creepers and weeds festooning the broken windows and doors. I had a sense of loss, that they had never been used since the British left.

Gathering up my newly acquired impressions and sensations to store for further thought, we continued on to see Chuchu's relatives, who are big landowners (sirdars). They own several villages which are dotted amongst large flat fields of padi, maize and vegetables. At the weekends they generally spend time at their farmhouse, making a break from their business life in the state capital of Chandigarh, some forty miles up the road. Here I was introduced to a group of charming ladies who were sitting outside on the lawn enjoying a mid-morning drink: grandmother, daughters, daughters-in-law and, of course, numerous grandchildren. Chuchu was warmly greeted, especially by her cousin Bohli, a lady of the same age, and there was much chatting and catching up on news, and enquiries about Rani.

I had been particularly interested and hopeful to make their acquaintance and have my first ever chance of walking round an estate village. After cool drinks and small eats, I was taken on a tour. Photographing as I went, I soon had an ever growing following of children, so excited to see pictures of themselves. What a happy time amidst grubby cows, snotty kids, shy mothers and extraordinarily large beehive-like structures, which I discovered to be mounds of dried buffalo dung pats, stacked ready for use as cooking fuel. Life in the village was feudal, but caring; a number of the young men and women from these villages entered into the sirdar's service, working either on the estate or at the large family mansion in Chandigarh.

Chandigarh has always been a very familiar name. Now a city of several millions and capital of the East Punjab, in my youth only a few dwellings existed. As for the Ghaggar River, where my parents had fished for mahseer while Colin and I had played, I looked down at this waterway in 2011 and saw only a stony beach with just a narrow trickle of water, men washing their trucks, and children playing amongst heaps of garbage. In fairness, however, I must add it was not the monsoon season.

The Chandigarh that met my eyes sixty-seven years later was certainly big and, I thought, somewhat shoddy and generally uncared for. There was so much litter, of course, but I was expecting more modern buildings and a semblance of greenery in a comparatively new city. It seemed there had been little attempt to beautify it either, at least in the centre of town, but driving out to the wealthy suburbs, the wide roads were tree-lined and the many private houses looked extremely prosperous, with high walls, elaborate wrought iron gateways, each with its guard.

Chuchu and I stayed a night at Bohli's mansion. A fleet of servants was awaiting us, although the family was still at their farm. Next morning, after a leisurely breakfast in the garden, we returned to Ambala. When I saw Reverend Bhatty, he told me he had found the relevant register and it was open for me to look at. So I took my camera and, standing on a pew in the vestry for a good overview of the document, I photographed all the details of the christening which had taken place on 15th November 1931. I had the satisfaction of emailing the pictures to Colin later.

Back in Delhi, there was one last visit to make before my departure: the Taj Mahal. At some ungodly hour Govind took me to the pick-up rendezvous where I was expecting to join a number of fellow travellers to Agra. Time went by and no one appeared. An hour later, I was getting pretty worried when a taximan asked for my ticket and told me that, as there were insufficient passengers for a bus, he was only taking myself and one other. The 'other' turned out to be a pleasant American Pole, so we enjoyed a roomy if hairy drive to Agra. There was a breakfast stop, thank goodness, before we raced on. Our guide in Agra was extremely pleasant, well informed and above all he didn't rush us or talk too much. He gave us a quiet resume of the history of the Taj and showed us where to get good shots. It was a Saturday and crowded, added to which we had arrived at the worst possible time on a very hot day of cloudless leaden grey sky – not a good backdrop for white marble. Beggars can't be choosers, however, and of course I had to go off piste and look for angles which encompassed some of the beautiful if few trees surrounding the tomb.

It is a truly marvellous work of art. The size, simplicity and site alone set it apart, long before you have time to study the exquisite intricacy of carved and engraved marble or the dimensions of the domes and four minarets. Once inside the tomb itself, there is not much time to linger. The walls are again beautifully decorated, and I picked out tulips and roses executed to the standard of botanical drawings, and all in white marble. Outside again and walking along a path, I came right back to earth with a sudden encounter. Two well kept and smartly accoutered bullocks were drawing a cart containing the fallen leaves and twigs surrounding the site. The driver obligingly stopped to allow me to record them.

Needless to say, I took a fair number of pictures – often thwarted by the appearance of unwished for figures, or groups with kids running around. Is there any angle that hasn't been tried? One of them might just be a winner! But there is a limit to even the most beautiful of objects and, because the Taj Mahal is so big, you cannot photograph 'bits and pieces' of it or try to capture 'twee' scenes. From the outside it's all or nothing.

We finally left for an excellent lunch, eaten in a pleasant garden where we were entertained by a small group of musicians from Rajasthan. This was followed by a visit to the factory in which the same beautiful inlaid marble is used to produce bowls, table tops, small jewel boxes and coasters. Exactly as in Shah Jahan's time, the craft has been passed down from generation to generation.

The last call was to Akbar's huge and very fine fort. There are palaces for himself, his son Jehangir (in pink sandstone) and his grandson Shah Jahan (in white marble). Towards the end of his life, Shah Jahan was over-thrown by his son Aurangzeb and imprisoned there, where he died some eight years later.

On one of my last days in Delhi, I spent a morning bird-watching with Chuchu and Rani on a lovely lake before the three of us indulged in a delicious Chinese meal.

The thoughtful kindness of Rani and her sister Chuchu was unbelievable. I spent two evenings with them during my stay, sharing their vegetarian meals and chatting. My B&B was within short walking distance so I didn't need any transport. Both women are so interesting and well read, real thinkers and very broadminded. Rani was widowed after only two years of marriage and later Chuchu, together with her daughter, Puja, joined her to live together in Rani's house.

16

While writing all these words, I have been mentally gathering together some vignettes, isolated descriptions of varying everyday scenes or occurrences I come across in my travels around Amman.

Visitors often comment on the cleanliness of smart, residential West Amman. Jordanians are as a whole quite oblivious of the rubbish they see, and certainly do not care in the least about throwing anything out of car windows, be it cans, plastic cups, bottles and paper. If questioned, the general assumption is that the orange-clad road cleaners will pick it all up. And they certainly do that, almost twenty-four hours a day. Some of the older men I have seen for years, working the same districts with poor implements, just a worn-down broom, a cardboard box, and a piece of wood to act as shovel. Others have managed to find a broken pram and adapt it as a cart. There are also those who work the rubbish trucks. They come by from early morning, sometimes twice a day covering the same route. Leaping off the back of the truck, the men skillfully swing the heavy metal rubbish bins onto the mechanical lift, and the contents are swept into a giant crusher. As the truck is revving up and moving on, they leap back onto the rear steps, hanging one each side ready for repeat performances all along the street.

Then there are the traffic police, both men and women. All are smartly dressed, and those women who follow the Islamic custom of covering the head will wear a white scarf with a hat or beret on top. Men on traffic duty can sometimes be seen wearing headgear similar to a shako, but with a spike instead of the plume, and a cotton piece to protect the neck. Traffic management, however, is not so smart. Hand signals are generally indecisive, even vague, and cannot be seen by most drivers. The great thing is the whistle. Blown almost incessantly, together with a gesticulating arm, you hope you've got the message to move forward across a road or squeeze round a roundabout with the addition of blaring horns, flashing headlights or simply cursing out of the window.

With some exceptions, gas is the method of cooking and this comes in large cylinders. Gas vans cruise the streets announcing themselves, each with its own brand of 'music'. This is usually a jumble of notes, often sounding like a run down or scratched record. One in particular has a ghastly rendering of 'Fur Elise'. If you want a new gas bottle, you open the window and shriek for the driver to stop. His aide will then heave out a cylinder or two and bring it up to you, taking back the empties.

At certain times of the year, other small trucks and vans will tour the streets. These are the hawkers and peddlers on the lookout for any jumble. Beds and broken sofas are particular favourites, worn carpeting, kitchen utensils, clothes – you name it they'll take it, after bargaining of course. I haven't actually dealt with these gentlemen, but getting rid of unwanted goods is no difficulty in a country with so much poverty. Clothes are one of the top priorities, especially shoes, and I give most of mine to charities or directly to any especially needy cases amongst the refugees.

Let's not forget the Post Office, where mail comes and goes and much is lost in between. Do not picture anything like a British institution with a stretch of glass-fronted counters. Let me take you through the glass entrance doors and then up a flight of steps to the first floor. Arranged there, are hundreds of adjoining metal boxes, painted green and each with a number and its keyhole. A narrow box some 18 inches long, 8 inches high and 8 inches wide, is where our mail is placed. If there is anything larger than a letter, it is simply crushed or squeezed in. Despite repeated requests for larger objects to be kept below and a note entered to that effect, everything receives the same treatment. Having retrieved your loot, you descend with considerable caution. The stair treads are narrow and covered in a badly fraying mock carpet. (I am glad to report that the stairs were eventually replaced entirely, in the local crushed marble mix.) At the counter (no glass) you can queue for one assistant, possibly two or, if unlucky, maybe no one. At my Post Office ladies predominate and most are scarfed. It is useful to speak to them in Arabic as on the whole anything beyond the pleasantries (a must), and postal requests, will not be understood. All that said, I am ever grateful for my Post Office box. How else would I obtain my mail except by begging to share someone else's?

What other gems can I add to this string? Ah yes! Supermarket shopping. Amman boasts some fine super-stores: large, clean, well laid out and richly stocked (in my view, too much so). The vegetable section in particular is a delight, with all shapes and sizes since we are not yet seriously into grading mode. Most of the veg are piled high in large containers, and all you have to do is take a plastic bag and rummage to your heart's content for those perfectly formed tomatoes, identical cucumbers, shapely green beans, matching red or yellow peppers, before moving on to the more delicate greenery like chives, beansprouts, rocket, parsley – all of which are thankfully wrapped. Everyday fruit, such as apples, oranges, bananas and grapefruit, also undergo rough handling. As for cabbages and cauliflowers, for sheer size many would win gold anywhere.

In the countryside things are a little different and generally more relaxed. I like to buy my vegetables and fruit while out on an excursion. It is fresh, particularly at the weekend, and there is always a lot of chat about where one comes from and how good one's Arabic is! The vendors, whether at the roadside or village stall, are so friendly that you often end up knowing all about their families and hearing the aspirations of their young men.

I travel a lot on my own and have occasion to drive along the same country roads many times in search of plants or pictures, or simply for the pleasure of being out in the open and away from Amman's noisome and hectic traffic. Bedouin or itinerant family groups will set up their tents often on the same patch of ground each spring, pasturing their sheep and goats and, if there is a piece of wasteland, sometimes cultivating it, remaining there until harvest time. As I pass them I wave and call out a greeting. Should they be eating, they will always shout an invitation to join them. With a further wave I shout back,

'Insha'allah mara tani' ('God willing, another time'). Offering hospitality is not only de rigeur, but extended in the most pressing manner – country people really like to have your company. The biggest drawback to all this kindness is the time such a visit will take. It is unthinkable to accept a glass of tea and then, after a brief stay, excuse yourself. A sense of time in the Arab world tends to be fluid.

* * * * *

Back from India, I found plenty of work awaiting me. The phosphate company (JPMC) was in need of further new stationery, business cards for their executive team and any other flights of fancy they might have. The major upheaval that year was the need to move house – yet again! With four very happy years in my then flat, I was suddenly informed that the lady who owned it had decided to up sticks, leave the United States where she had been working for more than twenty years, and return to Amman. Further enquiry elicited that she was of a somewhat unreliable temperament and given to changing her mind at the last moment. So I wrote her a friendly email and, knowing she also had another flat in town, I suggested she might like to live in that one and continue letting the other to me. I received a most stilted reply informing me that she intended to take back my flat and emphasized this by putting the words in bold. She was also under the incorrect assumption that I should be out by the June of that year. I hastened to correct this error as in fact my lease did not run out until the October. With upcoming long leave in the UK from mid July, there was barely time to find a new affordable apartment, pack up and move into it before October.

I literally scoured the town. Together with a most helpful driver from JPMC, we tried district after district, street after street, to no avail. There were delightful flats on offer, but 90 per cent of them were furnished and the others far beyond my pocket. Finally, and in desperation, with time fast running out to settle something before going to England, I agreed to take a basement flat at garden level in a different part of town. It was a big mistake, but I tried to make the best of it. The flat next to me was occupied by an elderly woman and her Indonesian maid. This granny had a son, his wife and four kids under eight who lived just below and rampaged all over my private piece of garden. When called to stop, they simply shouted in Arabic that it was not my garden; everything was theirs. They raced past my sitting room on roller skates, which was awful, and eventually I got my grumpy landlord to speak to their grandmother.

Parts of my flat were so dark that I needed electric light at all times and the view from my work room looked down on permanent lines of washing. But worst of all was the kicking of a football in that same area. At any time, especially during the summer months, and well into the night, these brats and invited friends just ran backwards and forwards shrieking and screaming, with the ball often crashing against the window bars. And no one except me said a dickie bird.

One October evening I returned from a visit and parked right outside the flat. Locking the car door, I tucked my bag under my arm and moved round the outside of the car to get onto the pavement. The street was not well lit but there was one lamp and, as I walked, a car crawled up very close to me and suddenly my bag was torn from my arm. I shouted out, 'My bag! My bag!', thinking at first that the strap had been caught on the car's door handle. The car raced off, turned a corner and was gone.

I had nothing but my car keys in my hand. I had just changed the lock of the front door and the new keys were not yet attached to the ring, so I couldn't get into the house. What to do? By the time the police arrived and took a statement in Arabic, entirely with the help of a kind young American couple fluent in that language, it was after ten o'clock. I rang my friend Diane, who I knew wouldn't be best pleased at that hour, since she has a very early rise for school. Bless her, she told me to come over and I stayed most gratefully that night, chez elle.

Next day, I called an Arab friend, Brahim, and he brought a boy to help him take the bar from a window in order to enter my house. The big question was, where was the spare set of keys? They could have been just anywhere, but thankfully I remembered putting them in a plastic bag in the bottom drawer of the sideboard. I explained this to Brahim and he found them immediately. Now at least I could get in. After that it was the usual procedure to report the loss of my ID card, driving license, money and my mobile phone, not to mention the vital address book and diary.

I had left the old flat early in August 1999, well before the due date. By December there was no sign of the owner, and from that day to this the flat remains empty, the shutters down.

Dear Colin and Anne, being at home and alone for Christmas and knowing something of my trials, invited me to come over. What a lovely, thoughtful surprise, which I immediately accepted. So mid December found me happily ensconced at 33 Salisbury Street.

Very shortly after my arrival, Colin became extremely unwell and had to spend my entire visit in bed. He was so low that I rarely saw him, let alone spoke to him. He just felt too poorly. Anne prepared a great Christmas lunch and invited some of the village 'waifs and strays' – folk who probably wouldn't be invited out or have that much money for a traditional meal. The weather was not conducive to any outdoor activities. The ground was frozen solid and terribly treacherous and we were glad to have a wood fire and be cosy. In any case Anne would never have left Colin alone. I flew back to Jordan early in January and poor Anne was already succumbing to the same ailment as Colin, which was eventually tracked down to be viral pneumonia – very nasty and lingering for them both.

Back at my pad, there had been some developments. The roof of the building, some four storeys up, had been sold to a wealthy Jordanian businessman living with family in the United States. He had come over to Jordan to supervise the building of a new apartment. Scaffolding had already been erected in November. My flat was below road level, and the first thing they did was to break the boundary wall and place boards from it to the apartment wall, just above my glass-fronted sunroom. I immediately complained, and was told it was only a temporary measure in order to gain access to the roof for building materials and cement. Of course it was nothing of the sort, and for four months the workmen wheeled barrowloads of cement to be raised to the top by pulleys. This caused an absolute mess of sand, cement, concrete chippings and general dust, damaging all my plants and leaving the windows spattered with a hard crust.

* * * * *

The news was getting around church friends that in March I was coming up to my eightieth birthday. Lex and June Macqueen (our church minister and his wife) decided to plan a special anniversary dinner party for me. You can imagine my surprise and pleasure at such a kind thought. The dinner was to be held at the home of the British Defence Attaché, Chris Rider, and his wife, Sabine. Apart from certain friends, I particularly wanted to invite the four secretaries whom I had known and worked with for so long: the two Mais from Princess Basma's office, Nada from the Mennonite Central Committee and Reem, the office manager at JPMC.

Then I had a great thought! Could I invite Princess Basma? If so, would she accept? How wonderful if she might just spend a short while to circulate among us. I approached one of the Mais and left it with her. Preparations went ahead for an estimated thirty-five guests, and then June took me to a patisserie to decide what kind of cake I would like – such generosity.

I had offered to provide the wine, and went to see my good friend Omar Zumot whose family own large vineyards in the north of Jordan. He actually manages them. He first made me sit down and taste some wines, then having chosen a case each of a red and a white I asked the price. 'There is nothing to pay,' he said. 'This is our birthday gift to you.' I was overwhelmed.

The date of the party fell exactly on my birthday, 13th March, and I waited hopefully for an answer from Mai. About three days before, she called me to say that the princess had a prior engagement, but would be delighted to drop by briefly that evening at around half past eight. Because of strict security the only people who knew about the Princess's visit were the Macqueens, the Riders and myself.

The great day arrived and I dressed up in a long purple skirt and matching purple and white-striped top, and brought out my beautiful amethysts – a necklace and pair of drop earrings. Then I drove over to the Riders' home. With a glass of Champagne, I wandered about in and out of the kitchen, offering any help, but was told firmly to go and sit down. By eight o'clock guests were arriving and soon the rooms resounded to laughter and chat. A little later I was standing near the front door to greet other friends. They were in a group and appeared to be a little impeded by a very large balloon. From behind this object a voice said, 'Hello Aunt Mink.' I was absolutely stunned, in fact quite speechless (a rare occurrence) for all of half a minute. Then when Christina's face appeared, I just shrieked 'Mini!' as we hugged. I really went bats and moved into the room shouting out, 'My niece is here! My niece is here!' Everyone must have wondered what on earth was going on, and why I was making such a noise. It was a fantastic pleasure and excitement – unbelievable to see a much loved family member simply appear out of the blue.

After I had calmed down and made further introductions, Mai came up and whispered that Her Royal Highness was due to arrive within the next few minutes. I alerted the Macqueens and Riders then descended the steps to greet Basma at the gate. We hugged each other very closely and then, arm in arm, climbed the steps. After the formal presentations were over, I took Basma inside to mingle amongst my friends. She was her charming self, chatting, laughing, smiling and putting everyone at ease.

Time moved on, and of course we couldn't start dinner before she left. I was just thinking how to manage this when Mai approached me and whispered, 'Her Royal Highness would like to stay for dinner.' With a quick word to Sabine, we shifted place names to prepare a seat of honour at my table. I had Basma on my right, and next to her Mini, together with Diane and Amal, the British Ambassador's wife. It was so unfussy and pleasantly informal, and certainly Basma wasn't concerned who sat next to her. That it was a buffet made the atmosphere even more relaxed.

During the course of the meal, Chris stood up and gave a short amusing piece about my indomitability, indefatigability and intrepidity. These words raised much laughter when it transpired that Chris was likening me to some of the Royal Navy's erstwhile aircraft carriers! So the evening progressed with many kind and amusing reminiscences, including words from Colin and Anne read by Mini, as well as her own thoughts.

Finally, when I was sure the speechifying must have concluded, Sitti Basma raised her arm and said, amid much clapping, 'Permission to speak?' She stood up and gave her version of how she remembered 'Ize' (her special name for me) in those early days of our association. As a teacher, I was sometimes likened to a 'dragon', but in later years to a friend. Finally, she added that one of the greatest gifts she had received from Ize was a love of reading. Who could ask for dearer friendship?

The evening progressed happily until our royal guest took her leave, followed by farewells from the rest of the party. Apart from the evergreen memories of that incredibly special evening, I received a folio filled with birthday wishes and pictures from friends all over the world. Anne had drawn a cover design depicting some of what she considered my achievements, including the accolades of Champion Cake Maker and Queen of Packers!

As a birthday gift Basma had offered me a laptop, a new PC or a television. I chose the new PC, which arrived at my Shmaisani flat and greatly cheering me up as the building noise continued and the dirt increased with liquid cement falling all over my plants.

During the course of that memorable evening Basma drew me aside and said she was so sorry to hear about the building construction. She said I really must move and that she would ask the two Mais to look around. By the end of March they had found a pleasant flat and they took me to look at it. I immediately liked it, and when all was settled I began packing up to move (the second time in nine months!). By the end of April, I was back on Jabal Amman and near my friends once more. Although a first-floor flat, it has a lovely glassed-in sunroom and there my plants have been undergoing rehabilitation.

55. The Taj Mahal, built between 1632-1653 by the
Moghul Emperor Shah Jahan in memory of his wife,
Mumtaz Mahal

56. A Lodhi Dynasty family tomb in
the gardens named after them, 2009

57. The lake in the Baluchi
Park Gardens, Delhi

58. The magnificent Amber Fort, capital of Jaipur until 1728, lies outside the city. Rajasthan 2011

59. Block printing on fabric at the Jaipur Co-operative Association, Rajasthan

60. Scraping water off a new carpet after washing, Jaipur Co-operative Association, Rajasthan

61. Family sunning themselves with their cow and dog, Bikaner, Rajasthan 2011

62. The highly decorated dining room at the Raj Vilas Palace where I stayed in Bikaner

63. A woman from the desert village of Khuri outside Jaisalmer, with her gold threadwork, Rajasthan 2011

64. Clothing displays in one of the very narrow streets of the Jaisalmer Fort, Rajasthan

65. Sample of a silversmith's wedding jewellery composed of a gold necklace and earrings inlaid with rubies. Jaisalmer

66. At Jodhpur market I came across this young man washing ginger. Rajasthan 2011

67. Also in the market, cobblers were busy at their trade.

68. The fifteenth-century Mehrangarh Fort. The many palaces within hold wonderful artefacts. Jodhpur 2011

69. I bought two small dhurries (cotton rugs) from this cheerful, friendly weaver when driving through the Ranakpur Valley en route to Udaipur. Rajasthan 2011

70. View of Lake Jangmandir from my hotel. It was on this island that the Maharaja of Udaipur once gave Shah Jehan sanctuary after defeat in battle. Rajasthan 2011

71. One of the hundreds of stalls at the annual spring fair held in Tughlabad, some miles outside Delhi, 2011

72. Mountain road in Oman, January 2013

73. Frankincense tree *(Boswellia sacra)* growing in the mountains of the Dofar region, north of Salalah, January 2013

17

2010 was a great year in Jordan for the flora and I spent as many days as possible recording them. From the pictures, I was able to make new handmade cards and enlarge some to be sold as prints. The JPMC calendar was underway, and in May I was very kindly invited to take pictures of the extensive and beautiful garden at Princess Basma's house.

Except for the area around the front of the house, the entire garden is on a slope. Beside the descending stone-flagged pathways, there are varying themes. I was enchanted with my constant discoveries of such a wealth of colour and design. Through rose arches were glimpses of brilliant annuals, or bottlebrush trees with their graceful flowering branches almost touching the ground. In contrast, as I came down to the lowest part of the garden, I saw an oval bed massed with more roses, blending colours, and so sweetly scented.

I had long been keen to try and use some of my photographs on coasters and place mats. Diligent enquiry, though, found no scope for producing such items in Jordan. So while I was on leave in England during the summer of 2010, I travelled up to Malvern to meet one of the best known manufacturers of such items. Malvern, in Worcestershire, renowned for its health-giving waters, is an historical city with a lovely abbey built on the high ground and surrounded by the Malvern Hills.

I stayed in a delightful Queen Anne B&B and next day met the director of the Coaster Company. Knowing nothing about the production process of coasters, nor about quantities and prices, I was quite nervous to meet Ken Beecroft. I had with me a CD of pictures I thought suitable for such a project, and he kindly had a coaster and a placemat made while we talked, so that I could picture what the finished articles might look like. Anyway, I left far better informed and began to think there might be a possibility of having some made to take back with me. It was a close-run thing since I was due to leave for Amman in three weeks. Having stuck my neck out, we began emailing and I sent the captions and approved the proofs with a tweak here and there. Ken had advised having twelve pictures made, it being a figure easily divided into several smaller quantities. I was very glad of that because it was exactly what happened.

Now I found myself with some three hundred coasters to sell, and twelve placemats as samples. Where to find room in my already overfull suitcase? A very kind friend who was flying later to Amman and who did not have either to weigh her luggage, nor explain its contents, put all my items in a small suitcase and handed them over to me in due course.

I was in the office of Princess Basma's private secretary sometime later that summer and showed her my newest production. She immediately asked me to leave them all for Her Royal Highness to see. She felt certain that there would be a lot of interest, and so it proved. Princess Basma passed the idea to her husband Walid Kurdi, Chairman of the Jordan Phosphate Mines, who placed a large order for both coasters and placemats.

Thrilling! But I was nervous as I set about placing the order and arranging for further proofs, writing the wording for captions, choosing the font, design and colour of boxes, deciding on the layout and printing of cover picture of each image, plus the company's logo – all conveyed by email. Payment was arranged but, due to incorrect addressing, the consignment was sent to Ann O'Neill and, not surprisingly, the shipping office had never heard of me. So there were nail-biting delays while the goods sat at the Queen Alia airport for days. They finally made landfall and thankfully were approved and, after repeated requests, I received a complete set of everything to grace my own dining table. I am glad to say that many visitors to JPMC have also been recipients.

18

Another plan I had been nurturing was a journey to Rajasthan. Diane had already been there and, unable to find a fellow enthusiast, I decided to go on my own. Once again it was emails all the way as I contacted the Indian travel agent in Delhi who had done Di and me so well in Ladakh and Kashmir during the summer of 2008. Having clearly stated my preferences, they prepared an excellent twelve-day tour around Rajasthan. I had a car and driver, and hotels and guides were included at every stop. All I had to do was keep my camera's battery regularly recharged and enjoy a part of India completely unknown to me.

First of all, however, I flew to Delhi and stayed at the same B&B as in 2009, within easy walking distance of my good friends Rani and Chuchu. Once again, a car and driver were put at my disposal by Mr Gupta, the managing director of the family-owned company Tradex. I later found that he had most generously paid for my accommodation.

With some days of leisure and pleasure in Delhi, I revisited old favourites like the Red Fort. There I found groups of young school children sitting in circles on the wide lawns. I asked a teacher what they were doing and he told me it was a lesson on Moghul history. The pupils had to write and draw something to describe their impressions of the white marble mosque of the Moti Mahal, so there was much sucking of pencils and picking each other's brains on what to say. They were only about eight or nine years old. With my camera at the ready, I hung over the low hedge and snapped. This immediately provided them with a perfect excuse to run over and ask me questions. So, after learning from one youngster that he liked the Moti Mahal but had forgotten who built it, I told him the story, by which time the whole group had joined in. Their English was fluent and their manners excellent.

The grounds around Humayun's Tomb are a delight and somehow magical, with their broken walls, enormous gateways often graced by the overhanging branches of beautiful trees, and in amongst the grassy areas other lesser tombs, all with connections to the Emperor Humayun. On another day I wandered along the paths of the Lodhi Gardens, which are always a pleasure, stopping to look at the newly planted flower beds: marigolds and snap dragons, yellow daisies and lobelias all massed in a delightful natural colour-clash.

One morning Chuchu, Rani and I went out to the Tughlakabad Fair. This huge outdoor event takes place every year for fifteen days in February among the lightly wooded sandy hillocks. Throughout this vast acreage, every region of India displays its wares. Foreign countries also participate, and I saw displays from Afghanistan, Bangladesh, Sri Lanka, Thailand and Vietnam, among others.

Sandals, dhurees, jewellery, carpets, printed skirts and blouses or filmy scarves in rainbow hues abound. So it goes on, each stall enticing and inviting. Not forgetting the hungry shoppers, in between all this are the coconut sellers, who with speed and dexterity split the shell and scoop out the succulent white flesh all ready for you to gorge. I spent a while trying to catch the key moments of this act. If you don't fancy coconut, as I don't, then go for freshly squeezed mango or pineapple juice. Sticky sweets like small crispy, elongated doughnuts or crunchy biscuits covered in sesame or poppy seeds are very 'moreish', and easily carried in a paper bag. Here and there you can actually sit, or rather push and shove to find a few centimetres on a bench. The key is first to establish ownership and then, leaving someone in charge, to go and queue for food at the so-called restaurants. By the time you return hot and frustrated from the bun fight, you'll probably find numbers have increased and granny is crouched over her soup and chappati where you expected to relax.

After those pleasant few days, I packed my bag and early on the morning of 12th February my car and driver arrived to start our journey – first stop, Agra. This was my second visit to the city and I still much enjoyed seeing the Taj Mahal, although rather briefly. One day I hope to see it on my own terms, away from the 'madding crowd' and early in the morning when the light is translucent. I had a most charming young guide, a Brahmin, who was to be married within days of my visit to a girl from a different caste, a Rajput. This was unusual, but the young couple had known each other from their school days and I had the impression that both sets of parents were educated and much more liberal than is normal in these cases. I kept up with Arousha who was keen to improve his English, and after his wedding he emailed me some pictures of himself and his bride.

The next morning we drove to Fatehpur Sikri, with its sixteenth-century sandstone palaces built by the Emperor Akbar, but abandoned some fifteen years later owing to the increasing population and lack of water in that desert region. It is a remarkable place, retaining so much grandeur and dignity after more than four hundred years of neglect.

My driver, Ajeet Singh, a Hindu, of swarthy skin and fine moustache, comes from Delhi, where he lives with his wife and two sons. Like so many hardworking people he is ambitious for the boys and somehow manages to send the elder one to a fee-paying school where English is taught at every level. Once we began the Rajasthan journey proper, I explained to Ajeet that we would not be driving non-stop, between 250 and 300 kilometres almost every other day. He wasn't quite sure what that meant, but soon got the idea as I frequently called 'STOP!', having spied water buffaloes wallowing in a pool beside the road, or to leap out to cross the desert sand and inspect a large flowering cactus bush. I was so fascinated by the beauty of its red flowers sprouting all up the stem that I took a close-up and the picture now hangs in my sitting room.

Rajasthan is not only the largest Indian state, but most of its area is covered by the ninth largest desert in the world: the Thar Desert. About halfway to Jaipur, a broken range of rough-hewn rocky hills appeared covered with straggly trees. I later learnt that these are of very ancient granite and known as the Aravalli Range. Flowering along the central reservation of our road were hundreds of vari-coloured bougainvillea, a beautiful sight in an otherwise rather plain landscape.

It is here in this seemingly inhospitable region that some of the most famous rajas and maharajas have through millennia lived, fought, built and created. Their history is a subject on its own. For a time, following Partition in 1947 and the setting up of the State of India, the maharajas still maintained enormous power and prestige, ruling their kingdoms as they had always done. With the advent of Indira Gandhi as Prime Minister, things changed irrevocably. These ancient ruling dynasties could join the Indian State and become an integral part of it, or face dissolution of their power, possessions and prestige. With few exceptions, they agreed.

In regard to Rajasthan (or Rajputana as it was known), this meant that the maharajas formed, as it were, their own federation with just one capital city, Jaipur. Today, while subject to Indian law, they continue to manage what are now called divisions. It has proved immensely beneficial to their subjects, since much of the wealth of each ruler is now channelled to social improvements across the board. Not only are funds expended, but the ruling families themselves are deeply involved with this transformation. Highly educated, widely travelled and interested in all aspects of new technology, the sons and daughters of the maharajas take great pride in the citizens' achievements.

Some four hours later we entered Jaipur with its crush of buses, rickshaws, scooters, carts, cars and of course, pedestrians, all jostling for road space. Piles of rubbish lay at the side of the road where bullocks and pi (feral) dogs rummaged, all cheek-by-jowl with glass-fronted shops or open markets.

Bissau Palace, where I stayed, is unlike other hotels in that it lies in the heart of the city amidst all the noise and dirt. But on the other side of the tall iron gates stands a charming place. Now a hotel, it belongs to the Bissau family, who are thakurs (landed gentry). Like all wealthy families, they had a town house. My bedroom door had a sliding bolt and was secured with a huge padlock. To myself I referred to it as a 'chastity belt'! The bedroom had a lovely inlaid tile floor, and above the wooden shutters a semi-circular window was lit by coloured glass.

In the afternoon Ajeet took me through the city jostle to visit the Rajasthan Textile Co-operative. There are a number of these co-operatives in different cities, all aimed at helping women in the rural areas to use their native skills and earn money. Material is provided, down to the silks and threads required for the production of embroidered cushion covers, delicate scarves, blouses and decorative wall hangers. The standard is high, and all work has to be examined and approved before it is put on sale in the co-operative showroom.

Don't imagine the co-operative to be a showcase. This one was in a high-ceilinged warehouse with bare electric bulbs, and little in the way of furniture except for the giant wooden trestle table standing in shadow at the far end. Here in this somewhat gloomy atmosphere are produced the most beautiful hand-printed cotton fabrics. The men who print them are not young; I imagine it takes many years of practice and experience to perfect what I watched them doing. The table was covered in its entire length by a piece of fine white cotton cloth. The printer, grizzle-haired and lined, held a large wooden stamp. Each of these stamps, hand-carved in teak wood, has the particular design required for that piece. Slowly, surely, perfectly accurately, entirely by sight, he placed the stamp along the edge of the material. Having completed the long strip, he then repeated this action down a second line and so on until all the cloth is printed. So far so good. That is only the beginning. With a different colour now on his next stamp, but exactly the same design, he has to repeat the entire process, perfectly covering the first stamp. By this time I was leaning over the table and very close to his hand as I photographed this action. With the stamp of course covering the first print, the only guide he had was to line it up with a small glimpse of an edge. And that was not the end. A third and maybe fourth colour would be added. (I have tried doing this with my rubber stamps, not very successfully.) The ink dries quickly and, after completion, the material is first given a short soak in salt water to set the dyes, and is then rinsed in cold water and hung up to dry.

Having taken my fill of this remarkable industry, I moved to another part of the building, here to watch all the processes of carpet weaving. It must have been about half past nine and still the weaver was working at his loom. He allowed me to get close to watch his dexterous fingers move the shuttle back and forth. Some wealthy client had given him a picture which he was copying. I then went to the back of the loom to photograph the array of bobbins from which the coloured threads make up the designs. Moving from the weaver to another carpet, I watched this one being checked for any fluff by an elderly man pushing a thin metal spike along every line of the weave. You would think that was that, but no. Nearby I noticed a young man, spotlessly turned out in this dusty atmosphere in a yellow shirt and mirror-shiny shoes. With what I would call sheep shears, he was meticulously clipping across the entire surface. As he brushed the loose wool away you could immediately see the difference; the clipped areas were much brighter, obviously free from any unwanted fluff.

At the final stage, a barefooted elderly man wearing only his lunghi (sarong) was pouring water all over a carpet. He took what looked like a spade with a turned-up edge and literally scraped back and forth across the surface of the carpet. After a further few sluices, he hung it up to dry.

So that was what went on downstairs. The men working here were craftsmen and received full-time employment and proper payment. I then climbed some narrow wooden steps and entered … another world. The huge area was divided into two sections: carpets and cotton fabrics. Unlike the semi-gloom downstairs, the whole place was brilliantly lit. Tea was offered while you sat and watched the carpets being rolled out. The manager told us whether they were woven in wool or silk or a mixture of both, and explained what some of the designs represented. They were breathtakingly beautiful and I took pictures. Some of the carpets were so large that I couldn't include the entire image in my view finder. Their prices, of course, matched their beauty and passed me by, but I was so keen for one or two to find homes that I entered into conversation with an Indian family and not only extolled their virtues, but did my best to persuade them to buy.

Later, at another warehouse, I did indeed buy. With prices this time within my range, I fell for twin rugs, each of an elephant design, and knew immediately that they would be for my great nephews, Tom and William. I also bought an all-wool rug with the internationally recognized 'elephant's foot' design.

But to return to the first co-operative, the walls of the other upstairs section were lined with shelves displaying rolls of fabric, and in front of them stood glass cases displaying the exquisitely embroidered silk blouses, scarves and lovely matching jewellery. I roamed among the shelves with a faithful follower ready to pull out any pieces I fancied, open them, and cast them over the cotton-sheeted floor for my admiration and inspection. It really was an overpowering experience – such a dazzling display. There were printed bedspreads, table-cloths of every size with matching napkins, place mats, table runners, cushion covers, pillow cases, all in this fine cotton and in a myriad of varying designs, the majority featuring either flowers, elephants or birds. I found a pretty tablecloth and asked for matching napkins. Within less than half an hour they appeared, all cut to size and perfectly hemmed.

Clutching my loot, I finally emerged about eleven o'clock, and Ajeet drove me back to the hotel. I must add one more detail about these co-operatives. Apart from the full-time employees, the salesmen are all volunteers, coming in after office hours and not only selling, but being extremely well informed about every aspect of the business.

Jaipur is a city of innumerable forts and palaces, probably the most famous being the vast Amber Fort which was once a private royal residence. Built on a hill some kilometres out of the town, the steep zig-zag road winds up to the top, and to get there you take an elephant. It was my first experience on the back of one of these beasts, and I have to say, a most uncomfortable ride. Sitting sideways on a hard seat with a metal bar to prevent you from falling off was not really my idea of fun. Where was the howdah? Elephants have such a huge rolling gait.

Having arrived at the fort, I spent most of the morning following my guide or turning off to look at some other architectural attraction, awed by the sheer size of the buildings and courtyards. Some of the individual palaces were for the royal ladies only and had delicately carved windows, their openings in the finest stone fretwork offering just enough space and light for the women to look out and watch proceedings going on below them. Many of the outer galleries were richly adorned with silver and mother of pearl over the entire domed ceiling and often the walls. Other walls were covered with beautiful floral frescoes, and the sandstone or marble pillars of every building were carved with flowers, demons or one of the gods.

Back in Jaipur, I toured the City Palace with its amazing collection of Rajasthani costumes, before visiting the renowned Jantar Mantar. The name is derived from the Sanskrit yanta mantr, meaning 'instrument of calculation'. The observatory was begun by Maharaja Jai Singh in 1728 and, before completing it, he sent observers to study foreign constructions. Each construction has a particular role; for example, measuring altitude and the position of the stars, or calculating eclipses.

Jaipur is also renowned for its gemstone market. One of the largest in the world, it deals in all the major precious stones. Late in the evening, Ajeet took me out of town to visit a diamond merchant – a friend of his, of course! Behind some ramshackle building I looked at the actual tools used for cutting the gems; unfortunately it was just too late to see the cutters in action. But then we went into the emporium, and what a blaze of light and glitter! All the jewellery on display was made there, and the pleasant, quietly spoken owner showed me whatever I wanted to see, explaining how the designs were created and how he catered for the many and varying tastes.

* * * * *

Leaving for Bikaner early on a grey morning, I managed to take some photos of camel carts, shops just opening, and a female road sweeper. We had about 170 kilometres to drive and I was excited to look out at the changing terrain, already knowing that Bikaner lay on the edge of the desert. I was immediately struck by the very strangely shaped trees. They were all over the landscape, in bright green fields, on sandy hilltops, and one standing quite alone by a brick wall and rubbish heap. Tall with thick, dark angular branches extended in a haphazard manner, it was the branch ends that intrigued me. They appeared to have large clustering tufts of leaves, which looked at first like mistletoe. Because of their height, I never got near enough to find out more and take some close-ups. No enquiries gave me any information and I am left thinking they must have been a type of acacia, a plant that would certainly survive the harsh desert climate in summer. The countryside is flat with a little mixed agriculture and frequent small brickworks. This is definitely camel country. Local transport of bricks and gravel is all drawn by camel cart, enormous sacks literally bulging to the ground.

Bikaner has a population half the size of Jaipur and it immediately shows. The roads are far wider. The traffic is far less frenetic. Flowers are planted in masses along the sidewalks, and cinemas abound. The city was founded in 1488 by Rao Bikar and was never captured. Being closer to Delhi, Bikaner spent more time fighting the Moghuls rather than other cities of Rajasthan, and the desert climate often brought defeat to its enemies. The main fort of Junagarh is surrounded by a long wall with more than thirty bastions. Within these walls are the palaces with their pretty courtyards, balconies, towers and windows, and what they may lack in size, they certainly make up for in art. I walked along passages, and through rooms decorated from floor to ceiling with really exquisite work: painting, engraving, carving on marble and sandstone, and beautifully in-laid floors. Around the tops of the walls were depicted scenes of hunting, one of the essential pastimes of the rulers. What really impresses one is the sheer detail, delicately painted rustic scenes, and floral murals, often portrayed using only a single hair on a brush. There seems no evidence of these arts dying out. There are always a number of young men and a few women to be seen in museums or at pavement edges, painting with the same detail and dexterity as their forbears.

The market was chaotic, as expected, very colourful and specializing in spices. This trade goes back hundreds of years to the time of the Portuguese when they occupied Gujarat. Spices were brought from the port of Kilanda and carried by camel caravan 600 kilometres across the Thar Desert to Bikaner which had the monopoly of sales. Business completed, the spices then began their long, long journey to Europe and, of course, to England. Caravans travelling west continued into what is now Pakistan, thence through Afghanistan, Iran, Iraq, the Ottoman Empire and finally by sea to their eventual destinations.

With the advent of British power in India, however, this route was considered too long and too dangerous, especially since the spices could now be easily shipped directly from Bombay.

Bikaner is also renowned for its shawls, scarves and carpets, like numdahs, the latter made from coarse woven felt. It was in the city that I took one of my favourite pictures. Rounding a corner, I saw a long, narrow alley-way and at the far end was a family sunning themselves outside their 'front door', that is, sitting on a wooden bench in the company of their cow and dog. Irresistible! A very large picture of them hangs in my bedroom.

I was really sorry to leave Bikaner. I mentioned camels earlier on, and these beasts were very much in evidence as they pulled their loads of bricks or huge sacks of fodder into their special market. In such a desert land, they are used almost exclusively for conveying heavy goods. The army which, I am told, has several thousand in its 'fleet', deploys them in the transport of weaponry and heavy equipment. It would make sense, and is a much cheaper form of transport. (On the North West Frontier of India, the regiments used camels as pack animals over mountainous terrain.) The city is also famed for its artists, especially their exquisite and detailed painting of eyes. It is interesting to find all this particularly refined culture so noticeable in probably the most 'desert' city of Rajasthan.

19

We had a long haul the next day, 303 kilometres across flat desert country to Jaisalmer. As usual, we made many stops and doing so I found four flowering plants, three of which I knew by name and the fourth also grows down in the Jordan Valley. Those strange twisted trees with knobbly ends to their branches continued to appear, but for the most part it was endless bare acacias and scrub. These acacias were originally imported, probably to help against soil erosion, but the authorities must rue the day, since they have now taken over vast areas of land and are extremely difficult to eradicate. I was becoming quite bored with this scenery when we suddenly came across a huge date plantation. I learnt that it is a new state venture. Full marks to them, in that hostile ground. I thought the whole layout very professional and the trees, although still fairly small, all looked strong and healthy. I never saw another plantation. Shortly afterwards, Ajeet pointed out a 'blue' jungle cow. They are quite wild and very shy so I was lucky to glimpse this one, alas too late to capture a picture. Called Nili Ghai in Hindi, it is smaller than the domestic beast, without a hump, and has blue/grey markings around its haunches.

Jaisalmer is said to have the oldest 'living' fortress in the world, housing some 4,000 souls within the many turreted sandstone castle built on an 80-metre-high prominence, which literally rises straight up from the desert plain. Founded in 1156, the fort is immense, with ninety-five bastions and measuring more than five kilometres in circumference. Inside the walls lives a thriving community and you find temples and havelis (merchants' houses), and endless quaint narrow streets housing not only the people but all their craft displays. What is most worrying for the castle dwellers is the pressure being put on their local community, and ultimately the fort itself, by the increasing number of hotels and eating places. These are exerting an enormous strain, not only on natural resources like water, but also on the overall structure of the fortress. Its inability to cope with the demands from the flood of visitors is very serious.

My budget did not cover a hotel inside the fort, and I stayed in the town below at the grandly named Lalgarh Fort and Palace. It is a new hotel, but leaves a great deal to be desired. My door had the same type of 'chastity' lock as in Jaipur, but the room itself was dark and at night was poorly lit. Going upstairs to find the restaurant, I came out onto a canvas covered area with a fine view of the entire fort. That was the best part. The restaurant itself was more like a quick snack eatery with tables under the awning, covered in cheap white cloths and badly laid. There were some groups who obviously took priority, and I had to call repeatedly for service. The fare was limited and not interesting unless you paid considerably more; I generally had vegetable spaghetti. In the morning it was worse, sometimes with no one around even at seven o'clock when most travellers are coming up for breakfast.

I wasn't there for long, however, and there was much to enjoy inside the fort. The two main walls are built without the use of either cement or water and have only one main entrance. It gives the impression of a frontier town, quite unsophisticated compared to anything I had seen so far. Between the sixteenth and eighteenth centuries its importance lay in being on the camel route which travelled between India and Central Asia. This brought great wealth, when merchants and townspeople built magnificent mansions all beautifully carved in wood and golden sandstone. These are the havelis which I had seen in Bikaner, but much grander and more elaborate, one or two still inhabited by the descendants of the families who built them. The rise of shipping from the port of Mumbai brought decline to Jaisalmer. With Partition in 1947 and the cutting of trade routes through Pakistan, Jaisalmer seemed doomed. The building of the Indira Ghandi Canal, however, has helped to revitalize the region.

The great doorway to the fort which forms the entrance was cunningly sited in such a way that it stands at an angle to the walls. This awkward turn made it impossible for any run-up in the event of an elephant charge. Within the fort are many extremely narrow streets, housing both inhabitants and their animals. During the day the owners drape their colourful wares along the walls. There are temples, of course, and a fine museum. From the ramparts you get an idea of the vastness of the Thar Desert with its scrub and sand dunes and, in the far distance, hundreds of wind turbines.

Knowing my interest in crafts, Ajeet took me one evening to visit an acquaintance who was a silversmith. We drove through a maze of streets and parked the car before proceeding on foot along narrow lanes beside monsoon drains. Together with the powerful smells of animal droppings and urine, mingling here and there with the sharp scent of incense, it was an interesting and sometimes hazardous walk in the semi-gloom, there being no lighting except from the houses. I bumped into cows several times. The passages didn't really cater for two-way traffic.

Arriving at the silversmith's, we entered a small room and I sat on a stool while he showed me the tools he uses and the designs he prepares for his jewellery. A necklace, earrings and bracelets are in great demand from prospective brides. It is surprising how much money the families are prepared to stump up for these pieces, very often to their financial detriment. The jewels are mostly rubies and sapphires with many small diamond pieces, often intertwined with gold thread.

Then we went upstairs, several flights in fact, passing various family members on the way, until we reached the holy of holies – his salesroom. Seated on the floor, I watched as he emptied bag after bag of stones and silver adornments, explaining their art – and value. It soon became clear that he viewed me not so much as a visitor, but as a potential customer. I didn't want to buy anything at that time and told Ajeet, but being India, 'no' was not an answer. So we moved to another room where I was shown some really old and beautifully decorated porcelain pieces which my host told me his great grandfather had acquired. I enquired about price; they were not for sale. Finally, after pouring out more bags of silver bracelets and getting no response, he grumpily led the way downstairs and we left on a brief farewell.

One afternoon I was taken by jeep into the desert proper, some 40 kilometres to a village called Khuri. I took a camel ride for one kilometre to climb the highest sand dune and, hopefully, watch the sun set. There were a number of other hopefuls, but we were unlucky.

Back in the village, I enjoyed myself just wandering around and taking photographs as well as meeting a jolly woman dressed in bright clothing and wearing countless white plastic bracelets all up her arm. Since she was of a fairly buxom build I was curious to know if she could ever take them off. 'Oh yes!', and she worked them all the way down her arm to prove it. There was an old man sitting and drinking milk from a gourd and boys playing cricket on the dusty ground, while goats and bullocks wandered here and there. The houses are round, built of dried straw and mud with thatched roofs which hang down a little over each building. Some are arranged around a small enclosed courtyard, and my eye was immediately caught by a young woman who was squatted on the ground, stitching beautiful gold thread embroidery. This is the kind of work which is done by rural women and sold in the co-operatives that I visited in Jaipur. It was a very pleasant interlude before the extremely cold drive back to Jaisalmer, with the desert wind blowing wickedly through the jeep's open back.

* * * * *

My next port of call was Jodhpur and this for me was the best of the stopovers. During the drive of some 265 kilometres we were in dense fog the first couple of hours and I was becoming depressed at the thought of seeing nothing. But the fog lifted and, although we were still on the edge of the desert, the land was slowly changing and becoming more fertile. Some 100 kilometres from Jaisalmer we stopped at Pokaran. In this desert town stands another fort built on a grand scale between the fourteenth and seventeenth centuries, this time in plum-coloured sandstone. I wandered around the walls and into the museum, which consisted of endless paintings of the various maharajas and also some of their armaments and brocaded clothing. It was quite deserted except for an Indian family and the chowkhidar (guard). Pokaran is also noted as being the site for India's nuclear tests in 1998.

Jodhpur is the second city of Rajasthan, but with only about 1.4 million inhabitants. Its name is, of course, closely associated with the erstwhile fashion of wearing jodhpurs for riding. The streets are really wide and pretty clean. My hotel, Ratan Vilas, was built in 1920 by Maharaj Ratan Singhji, a royal from Jodhpur and a noted polo player. It was converted into this charming hotel by his son and grandson, both of whom live in part of the house where you may wander at will and enjoy looking at the beautifully decorated walls and ceilings, the gracefully carved furniture and the pictures of family members. They make a point of meeting their guests regularly. Unluckily I was too early at breakfast and missed the visit.

Turning off the tree-lined street and driving down a short way you meet a delightful building, with a gentle fountain playing in the midst of a large grass lawn, brilliant bougainvillea growing up the pillared entrance, a swimming pool and the sound of birds. The moment I stepped into the hotel I was relaxed, and so it continued throughout my sadly short stay. My room was off an open courtyard; it was quite simply furnished, with yellow silk covering the comfortable bed, and some black and white family photos, but so peaceful. Meals were taken in another open courtyard with a chequered floor. Around the balcony above were other suites.

Next morning dawned warm but somewhat cloudy as we set off first for the Jaswant Thada. This is a group of mausoleums situated near the special cremation site for the maharajas. All built of white marble, the centre-piece is a really beautiful temple which was erected by the widow of an earlier maharaja. Since Hindu temples are forbidden to be near cremation sites, this has been turned into an art gallery. Everything is on a grand scale, as so often, and standing within green lawns and neem trees, it is literally 'a picture'.

Then up the winding road to the great fifteenth-century Mehrangarh Fort, a marvel of engineering. Certainly one of the most impressive and formidable structures in Rajasthan, it stands on the hill above the town and is virtually impregnable. Within this huge edifice there are some forty palaces, each housing fabulous collections of royal trappings, interior decor, carved panels and delicate latticed windows, the latter all in sandstone. As you climb ever higher, there is one interesting feature to look down on: Blue Town. It is an old town area of Jodhpur and it is blue. The story behind this unusual colour lies, as so often, in history. This was the original town built within the fortified walls surrounding the fort, and had four gateways. In times of unrest, Brahmins, the priestly caste of Hindus, were often at risk of attack or religious infighting. They painted their houses blue to distinguish them from others and as years went by the townspeople, finding the colour a cool relief from the harsh light of the Thar Desert, decided to do likewise.

* * * * *

So on to the final leg of this journey of discovery and the one over which I lingered as long as possible. We were going to cross the Aravalli Hills, now to become a very important part of the landscape, but before that, we had the lovely drive along the Ranakpur Valley. From the moment we left Jodhpur I had noticed a different terrain, albeit still desert. There was a greater variation of scrub and along the road bright yellow flowering bushes, which I think are a species of Colutea (senna). Lone rocky outcrops appeared across the desert floor, before we turned off the main highway and took a quieter route. Almost immediately we were in a fertile belt with hamlets nestled beside the river, alongside fields of sugar cane and other crops. Beautiful tunnels of tall, graceful neem trees arched over the road. Looking at my photographs, I never cease to enjoy the blue of the sky seen through their delicate leaves. Before leaving the valley, I stopped to look at the fifteenth-century Jain temples. The central one is very large indeed with every possible surface carved or engraved with Jain images. There are twenty-nine connecting halls, supported by 1,444 pillars and, with one exception, each is carved differently. Quite something.

In complete contrast, I soon stopped at a weaver's home. His mats and dhurries were displayed beside the road and I was quickly met by the jolliest of artisans. He spoke remarkably good English, not common in such areas, and proceeded to throw down his selection of wares. I could have bought several straight off but, as usual, had to be realistic! I took two and then my friend went to his loom, and proceeded to continue on a current job while I took pictures. Suddenly he put his hands to his head, gave a smile and disappeared. Seconds later he reappeared with even bigger grin and I saw he was wearing his turban. Without it he had definitely felt undressed.

As we climbed higher, the terrain became more rugged and challenging. Gone were the fields and grazing animals. The peaks of jagged rocks descended steeply into jungle-like valleys, their slopes dotted with many dead or dying trees and littered by boulders and creepers. Because of the haze and lack of colour, it was very difficult to take any pictures. What we did come across, though, were monkeys. I had forgotten all about them and unwisely let down my window – a little. In seconds they were swarming all over the car, skinny arms even thrust through the narrow opening. Ajeet shouted at me to close up, so I took a picture or two from inside the car before we drove on. That was the only time we saw them.

At the summit we stopped at a very pleasant roadside restaurant, where I enjoyed a simple meal outside and talked to a party of English tourists heading in the opposite direction. They were rather surprised to see me travelling on my own and wished me a safe journey.

Descending the hills into a landscape of rural husbandry, I took pictures of timeless India: country life, with its simple dwellings, children, dogs, fowls and neatly stacked roundels of dried dung. Young girls were spreading their washing on the warm rocks above the nearby river. Best of all was to watch paired oxen slowly turning the water wheel and raising the water to the channels for irrigation of the fields, in a practice going back thousands of years. In one village Ajeet stopped the car to point to a very tall tree. On it were scores of fruit bats, just hanging asleep until the sun went down and they could go hunting – something I had never seen before.

From now on the scenery became rather dull and the flat land was again dotted with small brick factories. Finally we arrived in Udaipur where the Incentives representative had almost given up on me. I had taken twice the usual journey time and completely forgotten he had booked a boat ride that evening. I had been far too interested and engrossed in the journey and didn't mind too much missing out on that trip.

The hotel was very poor (as I reported to the company). It was well sited on the lake but, as I soon discovered, undergoing a complete renovation so that there was neither restaurant nor food, other than room service for breakfast. The staff were fairly offhand; with only myself and an Indian family in residence, they obviously didn't care too much. That meant finding somewhere to eat each day.

The write-up on Udaipur is almost lyrical, describing its fairy-tale palaces and lakes, but apart from a boat ride around one of the manmade lakes and a drive with Ajeet along another, I was definitely isolated from the life of the city. My guide took me to the City Palace, perched on a hill overlooking Lake Pichola. Like other palaces it houses some very fine artefacts, including a remarkable collection of miniatures and some beautiful mirrorwork. The Durbar Hall was originally named after Lord Minto, Viceroy of India, who laid the foundation stone in 1909. It is really grand, with immense chandeliers and a seating capacity of several hundreds. Running round the top floor are the viewing galleries where the veiled women could watch the proceedings in privacy. The hall now houses an amazing collection of rare crystal ordered from England in 1877 by the Maharaja. He died before it arrived and it was never used, remaining in boxes for one hundred and ten years. The collection includes tables, chairs, sofas and beds as well as a jewel-studded carpet. Photography was strictly forbidden so I couldn't record even one piece of this incredible display. Lake Palace Hotel, one of the most luxurious and costly in the world, is built on a small island on the lake and was originally the home of the maharajas. Needless to say, you are not allowed to land there unless you are a guest.

Apart from a drive around the lake with Ajeet before my departure, it was a rather disappointing end to an otherwise fantastic journey, and I was glad to take the road to the airport for a flight back to Delhi. Always optimistic, however, I still caught some fun pictures of life along the highway and concluded with a shot of one of the exotically decorated trucks.

In Delhi, I enjoyed further sightseeing and time spent with Chuchu and Rani. One of the joys was revisiting the Midland Bookshop, browsing and finally selecting some books; this time choosing authors whose names were known to me, but whose pages I had not read. This is always a gamble, especially for someone steeped more in history, travel and biography than modern writings.

I paid a second visit to the Lodhi Gardens and watched a large mixed group of school children enjoying a visit. Like all youngsters, they rushed around, the girls giggling, the boys yelling, and all of them throwing away their sweet bags until the grass was littered. Presently, some of the girls drifted over to me and we started talking. I was impressed not only by their English and good manners, but with the wide range of subjects we chatted about. They answered my queries without coyness or silliness, and in turn asked mature questions. When the whistle blew they said goodbye and rejoined the others. I stood and held my breath – would they leave all their rubbish and walk off? There was still a lot of horseplay and noise as staff gathered their flocks. Then one or two teachers handed out large plastic bags and immediately everyone was busy picking up the litter. Within minutes the grass was green again, boys and girls lined up, and away they walked, some of them waving to me as they passed by. Was I happy! Jordan, take note!

20

The spring of 2011 in Jordan was poor. With no rainfall before the end of 2010, the land grew desperately parched, added to which we suffered from frequent strong drying winds. I drove countrywide in search of the usual array of flora, but much of what I did come across was wind-damaged, with leaves discoloured and the flower petals badly torn. In some cases, certain species hardly appeared.

The King Talal Dam is probably one of the clearest indicators of drought. One year, the Zarqa River which feeds the dam was at very low ebb. The lack of water feeding into it and the constant demand from the Jordan Valley farmers for crop irrigation had left a shoreline of cracked mudflats either side – a very sorry sight.

This year, 2013, in complete contrast, we are almost 'drowning' in water. It is many, many years since I have seen such weather conditions in Jordan. Even as I write, the rain falls non-stop following a night of sleet and snow. The dams must be singing their hearts out and I cannot wait to go and look at them.

I think this is a good moment to digress again with some more of my 'local' observations. I have already mentioned the stalwart orange-clad street cleaners and dustbin emptiers. But there are others who are always interested in the bins. These are generally solitary men who roam the prosperous tree-lined streets of private flats and houses. Daily I see one or two stop by the large steel bins opposite my flat and literally go through everything: tins, cardboard boxes, wasted food, clothing, electrical parts, toys and, of course, scrap metal. They will spend a considerable time sorting out their choices and then bag them up and move on to the next possibility. I have come to recognize one or two and we exchange smiles if I am down in the street. I often wonder what they do with it all; I am sure it is recycled one way or another to give them just about enough money with which to feed themselves. They probably sleep rough and have no proper accommodation.

There is a woman I wave to each time I pass, where she sits with her knife grinder. When I first saw her she was young and very pretty, with a baby at her breast. I gave her some clothes and learnt that she was Egyptian with a husband who has occasional work as a road labourer. About every fifteen to eighteen months she appeared with another baby, and I once took a photo of the then family of four. Now, some twenty years later, there are at least eight youngsters, with the eldest boy often sitting at the wheel. Occasionally I see someone having their knives ground, and have also learnt that a wealthy businessman drops off food on a regular basis.

Then there are the street vendors at the traffic lights. Items on offer change with the seasons. Now with spring upon us, we can buy bunches of tulips, irises, freesias, roses, or a box of strawberries straight up from the Jordan Valley – delicious. When these finish, it is time for balloons, bubble blowers, cheap squeaking toys, kites and cowboy hats. Autumn and winter bring flowers back again, this time with chrysanthemums and potted euphorbias; also sweetmeats like nougat, and sesame biscuits, as well as Islamic calendars and, of course, more plastic toys. I have to say that the flowers are always fresh and very well packaged. I generally buy from these men who are considerably cheaper than any shop.

For a complete change, you can sometimes see a shepherd guiding his flock across the street and onto a patch of land, where the animals quietly graze, gradually moving along, but always just behind the donkey. I looked out of my window very recently and saw just that sight. So you see a variety of ways of living, and all are there to add to your interest and knowledge.

Back to the dams … in spring of this year, 2013, I finally went down to the King Talal Dam, keen to inspect the amount of water and take a coffee with my engineer friends. Musa told me that, despite the immense amount of rain we had had this winter, the dam was only just over half full (40.4 million cubic metres). I could see for myself that there was still a noticeable high water mark well above the present waterline. Elsewhere, in other dams, water levels were reasonably good, and along the deep gorge of the Heidan River the rare white hollyhock was well out, growing side by side with very tall yellow fennel. Down at the water's edge, the oleanders were bursting into mass bloom amongst the rocks, set off against a clear blue sky.

This year has also been good for the famous black iris. It is considered to be the national flower of Jordan and I am repeatedly asked when it flowers and where to find it. It turned up trumps and I have made several excursions with friends to show them this lovely flower and explain some of its characteristics. Because we have other equally striking wild irises of a similar hue, for visitors it can be frustrating to find themselves looking at the wrong plant.

Sadly, however, the flora overall was again disappointing. The continuous rain and strong winds did so much damage to cyclamen, anemones and red buttercups in particular. As the days grow warmer grass comes up very quickly and soon the wild flowers become hidden.

There was one area where I much enjoyed working. With the many dark days and heavy clouds I used to take the car and, regardless of weather conditions, just drive out to a favourite spot in the hope that there would be no rain. This was often the case once away from Amman, and the stunning skies would suddenly appear. I had to work quickly, and became over excited by the sheer beauty of the landscape. I did take some striking pictures, and I always hope that viewers may love them as much as I do.

To try selling more pictures and become better known, I took a small booth at the Souq Fann (Art Souq) in Amman. I didn't sell very much, but I learnt a lot and enjoyed meeting all the young men and women around me who were also trying to promote themselves. The nineteen-year-old boy next to me was studying engineering in Jordan and loved drawing. I was most impressed with his work, all in pencil. His parents and other relatives came to see him and he insisted on introducing me to them all. His mother is Bosnian, a charming and talented lady. I also exhibited a collection of photographs at one of the cafés in a street with many eateries and very popular amongst tourists.

Jubilee Year, together with the Olympics, brought growing excitement in Britain. I commemorated my own jubilee, celebrating fifty years since I first came to Jordan. I have witnessed so many changes. Regretfully, my work with the Jordan Phosphate Mines Company has come to an abrupt close with the resignation of the Chairman/CEO who had been my boss. Within Jordanian society there has been a noticeable growth in population, architectural styles, land encroachment, incredible increase in road traffic and road construction, modernization of stores and building of many unnecessary malls. Very sadly in this respect, I am observing a decline of the old style shop. Recently I went to a small village-like street I had used for many years, only to find that the little supermarket had gone and had been replaced by a foreign bank, the newspaper shop gone and replaced by an expensive jeweller. On the positive side, there has been much tree planting and a slowly growing awareness that Jordan must take care of its natural heritage and overall environment.

In this respect much credit must go to the Royal Society for the Conservation of Nature. I have been associated with it for many years, producing handmade cards from my floral photography. The Forestry Commission employed me to travel the length and breadth of the land, recording all the trees (indigenous and imported) – their trunks, bark, leaves, flowers and seeds – throughout the season.

All new environmental projects interest me, particularly anything to do with plants and conservation. I continue to study the flora, and never cease to be thrilled by its beauty, structure and adaptability. I would dearly love to produce a coffee-table book on my pictorial and written observations throughout my long years in this land.

I continue to work with Iraqi refugees and also regularly visit some very sick Jordanian ladies. Now, we are witnessing the unbelievable horrors of mass killing in neighbouring Syria. A country so steeped in history, so beautiful, it is almost impossible to picture the destruction, not only of lives, but the loss of its integrity. As I write in 2013, numbers of Syrian refugees in Jordan alone have reached more than half a million.

As always, I planned a summer visit to the family, and this year was to be very special with the addition of Johnny and Jenny from Vermont as well as Christina, Harry and the boys. We were celebrating the forty-first wedding anniversary for Colin and Anne, and Colin's upcoming eighty-first birthday in September.

On 12th June I received a call from John Millar, a close neighbour and good friend of the family. He told me very simply that Colin had died earlier that day. I was stunned and just sat in my chair doing nothing, feeling dead myself. I had missed seeing my dearest brother by eight days and simply couldn't imagine 33 Salisbury Street and Cranborne without him. I thought of dear Anne – what she must be going through, and of Johnny who had missed Colin by just five days.

I arrived in England on 20th June and the following day we held a private family funeral for Colin as he was laid to rest in the churchyard of Cranborne's ancient church, where he had worshipped and offered the chalice at Communion for so many years. He lies in a beautiful spot just below the tower, to the top of which he had climbed many times to hear the clock strike midnight for the New Year.

Johnny and Jenny had to fly back to the States very soon and we arranged another date for Johnny to return again for the service of thanksgiving. Such a tough time with so much grief and heartbreak. Christina throughout was an absolute tower of strength to Anne. We settled down with less than one month to plan the service and on 11th July, with Johnny back once again, we held the most beautiful commemoration of Colin's life in hymns, readings, music and joyful remembrances of his career and his love of family. The church was packed with many from the village and surrounding areas – Colin was not only a very familiar figure, but much loved for his friendliness, kindness and humour.

We had a piper from the Orkneys, who despite thirty plus years living in Dorset and married to an English woman, still had the broadest of accents which even Anne could only partially understand. The Wilton Hunt, which Colin and Anne had unswervingly supported, sent huntsmen and two hounds to stand either side of the south door of the church. Afterwards we all gathered in the village hall where so many friends and relatives could mingle.

I returned to Amman in late summer and life continued on its course with autumn and Christmas still to come. I began my annual preparation of Christmas cards, something I really enjoy. With orders coming in, I was much encouraged and spurred on to complete them in good time.

In November Lex and June, our minister and his wife, approached me with the suggestion of joining them on their two-week trip to Oman. The previous November, I had spent just five days there and had told myself, with somewhat wishful thinking, that I must return. So it was that on Christmas Day following a cheerful lunch party, we three set off for the airport and a flight to Muscat via Bahrain. It was early morning when we touched down at Muscat and took a taxi to the Delmon Suites, where we had booked in for a few nights.

After a rest and breakfast we picked up the four-wheel drive and took ourselves down to the corniche over-looking the Sultan Qaboos Port. This inner harbour is fairly small, specifically accommodating the Sultan's magnificent yacht, El Said, and a flotilla of lesser vessels. Beyond is the shipping port. The setting of the corniche itself is a long, curved sea wall, the pavement laid with attractive coloured stones. The gazebo-like domed open shelters allow one to sit and enjoy the view. The road running behind is dual carriageway and the wide central reservation is planted with a brilliant display of multicoloured petunias. Date palms complete the picture, and you may imagine my delight and frequent requests to stop!

We strolled in and out of the seafront shops crammed with real oriental items: patchwork and sequin cushion covers from Rajasthan, and pashmina scarves, carved wooden elephants and embroidered bedspreads from Kashmir. The traditional Omani men's round embroidered caps, known as kuma, were everywhere, and I bought two for my great nephews.

Later, we explored a bit further to look at the old part of Muscat. The streets wind up and down, edging the mountains, which are literally nextdoor neighbours. Set behind high white walls, the houses in general are less than three or four storeys, giving glimpses here and there of green lawns, vibrant colour and, of course, date palms. The impression is one of tranquillity.

Next day we decided to take an open-top bus tour. Given earphones and excellent commentary, we were taken through the city and out along the coast, passing some very fine official buildings; the Royal Omani Police headquarters (more like a royal residence) was set in landscaped grounds. With my recently acquired smaller camera, I was crossing from side to side upstairs, intent on catching all possible views. The earphones had little chance and I missed quite a bit of information. We drove along the seafront, the dazzling azure water lapping gently at the fine sandy beach. On the other side of the road I saw, for the first time, mangrove swamps. I thought the trees were rather small and insignificant, not at all what I had imagined, but they form an important part of the ecology, protecting the coastal areas from erosion. Passing the yacht club and the famous Al Bustan Hotel, we returned to Muscat rather better informed.

Early the next morning we left for the journey to Nizwa, the ancient capital of Oman. Our destination was the Majan 'camp', a few kilometres outside Nizwa. We didn't really know what to expect but the compound, with its small individual huts, was quite acceptable. The walls and roof of each hut are faced with bamboo and inside, the beds were comfortable and the water hot. There was no garden as such, but a playground for children which was brilliantly lit at night. The whole area around us was just sand and scrub with mountains hovering not far off. I was intrigued to note the type of protective fencing. It consisted of shortened lengths of dead date palm trunks placed closely side by side forming a palisade.

We sortied from there next day to take a mountain road and explore one of the high valleys and get real views of the ranges. It was somewhat misty, but we were duly impressed by the grandeur and the endless line of sharp peaks standing out against the sky. The overall colour is grey and, although there was some vegetation, it merged in with the scree and sandy gravel everywhere. We picnicked amongst the rocks and I wandered off to look for plants. There was not much up, but it was January, the start of the short spring season, and here and there I saw some tiny flowers and a sprinkling of leaves. There are, of course, some bushes which survive the heat, but they do not grow fast. Temperatures reach at least 48°C in summer so it is best to hunker down. We were joined by a group of goats who obligingly finished off the remains of our meal. They were rather an attractive sandy colour. It was from here that we had a clear view of Jabal al Shams (Sun Mountain), some 3,000 metres and the highest in Oman. That evening we partook of a simple meal at the camp restaurant and prepared for the next day.

For years I had listened to friends describing the uniqueness of Jabal al Akhdar (Green Mountain), the large mountainous region with its notable vegetation. So it was with considerable expectation that we began the drive up and round the snake-like bends. We made numerous stops. Here I saw Sodom's Apple (*Calotropis procera*) as well as Dodonea viscosa. Both these shrubs are found in Jordan, but the first grows only in the heat of the Jordan Valley and the second is frequently planted as a hedge in Aqaba. This leads to my conclusion that, despite the altitude, these plants flourish because of the extremely high temperatures almost year round.

On another occasion, we explored Nizwa itself, especially the older parts. The souq is very inviting with its many ethnic craft items, and the covered and marble-floored vegetable market is spotlessly clean. Later we visited the fine seventeenth-century Jibreen fort, hoping to get a look inside. Being Friday, though, it was closed. It seemed, however, that I had attracted the attention of three young women, all in black – as per tradition. They were absolutely fascinated by my white hair and insisted on being photographed with me, giggling and clutching my arm. Speaking Arabic certainly helped and I now have a record of this event!

The next major jaunt was a flight to Salalah, far south and close to the Yemeni border. Salalah is Oman's main port, the city very well laid out, the dual carriageways lined with coconut palms and, like Muscat, brilliant with floral colour.

The area of the frankincense tree (*Boswellia sacra*) is found within this region of Oman in the Dhofar mountains. I was eager to see these trees, and even more so when I discovered in what harsh conditions they grow. Dotted haphazardly about the mountainsides, they are often high up and difficult to approach over the loose rocky terrain. The tree itself is rather untidy, with a rough, peeling bark and groups of deeply curling leaves. The small creamy flowers appear in a branched spray. Frankincense is tapped from the scraggly but hardy trees by slashing the bark, which is called striping, and allowing the exuded resin to bleed out and harden. It has been traded on the Arabian Peninsula and in North Africa for more than five thousand years.

I was amazed to discover how many types and qualities of incense are derived from the sap, with equally varying prices. One tends to think of its use in church services or other religious rites but it is also an important ingredient in the perfumery business.

With its vast expanses of barren desert, Oman is a large and extremely mountainous country. In amongst these regions you find many towns of varying populations as well as grouped farming communities. The mainly white dwellings standing amongst the dark green of palm groves are an attractive sight, especially those with a backdrop of the sea.

Our return journey from Salalah to Muscat was around one thousand kilometres and we stopped at four different rest houses en route. Most of the driving was through desert – the first time I had experienced such vast expanses, and I tried to picture myself doing it on camelback! I should like to return yet again to Oman and concentrate on special places, with leisure to study the plant life further.

As I mentioned at the beginning of this chapter, 2013 in Jordan began with incredible amounts of rainfall – more than recorded at any time. The result was disastrous in many urban areas where water from the storm drains, unable to cope, simply overflowed through the streets with such violence that much in its path was overpowered and swept away. Hundreds of homes were flooded and sadly there was loss of life.

At the end of that first week, snow started to fall with freezing conditions and utter chaos on the roads. Returning from the airport, we saw vehicles strewn everywhere and a journey usually of thirty minutes took almost two hours. If life in the rural and urban areas was hard, then picture the misery for thousands of Syrian refugees living in a tented camp in the desert of north Jordan.

January moved slowly into February, and I began to look around the countryside for signs of spring. True to form, the delicate pink flowers of the almond trees were appearing. There are many wild ones and these, blossoming amongst bare trees, are particularly lovely.

After the heavy rains, my next trip was down to the King Talal Dam. I learnt that it had risen to sixty million cubic metres, a must to see as it was more than ten years since anything like that figure had been recorded. I went down to see for myself and was not disappointed.

* * * * *

The years have rolled on since I first came to Jordan on a snowy night in 1962. There have been so many changes, so much urban expansion, sadly not always wise or even necessary. The hunger for land is very strong in Arab peoples and it seems, once you have your piece, the most important thing is to cover the maximum area with concrete. Little thought is given to environmental suitability – high-rise appearing beside two-storeyed villas. Alas, noise abatement is an unknown subject and the unending hooting of vehicles, screech of brakes or engine-revving on a sports car as it races up and down the empty roads at night, continues without check. In comparison with other Arab countries, I feel sad about our continuing noise pollution and lack of road discipline.

There is much kindliness among Jordanians and I have shared such good times with all sorts of people. Recently, I left a favourite patterned shopping bag at Fouad's Supermarket. I called and asked them to keep it until I came by. Days later when I went to the shop it couldn't be found. Disaster! While they were searching, the owner apologized and I brightly suggested that in lieu of the bag I might take groceries for free. 'You are most welcome,' he replied, and I knew it would be so. But when the bag finally turned up, I joked with him in mock sadness, saying, 'No free groceries now!' Together we had a good laugh, with others soon joining in. That conversation took place in English, but in the countryside where Arabic is really necessary, even with my poor version, you can still have many a laugh. It may be over my language, or perhaps I comment on a pretty daughter and the family ask me to find a rich husband for her. There is such a feeling of camaraderie, you finally drive off with warm farewells and 'Insha'allah binshufak maratani!' ('God willing, we'll see you again'). And this could be in the middle of nowhere.

I have found great joy in all kinds of places, but landscape the world over has been my inspiration and a great driving force. I never cease to be overwhelmed at the majesty of creation, shades, shadows and desert shapes, the unending variations of green, exquisite plants no taller than the heel of your boot, or mountains holding fathomless pools of hushed waters beneath a mercurial sky. I cannot ever forget clouds; they give substance and character to many a picture. My friends laugh when they hear me say that. They know that my mind's eye is far away – thinking of what I may find – over the hills.

On 13th March 2014 I shall be 84. Time to close my story. My life has been full of adventures and I have been greatly blessed by my family, my friends and, not least, by the people whose hands touched mine wherever I have lived and travelled. I have no wish to go to the moon. This earth of ours, so stunningly beautiful, so kind and gracious, so generous in its gifts, I can never see enough of it.

I hope there will be other journeys – a slow boat along the Brahmaputra, a return to Kashmir, or a unique chance to see the magical flowering in the desert of Namaqua National Park. But that is another story.

In Praise of
The Gun Smoke Still Lingers

Ann O'Neill has written a remarkable and fascinating account of a life lived through times and in places all around the world seen with the eyes of someone with indefatigable optimism and a generous spirit. The child of an Indian Army officer, her early life was a kaleidoscope of short visits and postings to different places ranging from the North West frontier to a jungle camp in South India. It seems to have been idyllic, but it must have also been tough. At one point while her father was hunting bears, her mother had to cater for the family in a snowbound hut with only a packet of macaroni and a Primus stove! But in the spirit of the times such things were overcome with uncomplaining fortitude and this attitude has stood Ann in good stead throughout her life.

It shines through in her accounts of the struggle to live and work as a single woman in Amman. She became a presenter at Jordan Television and Radio Jordan, and on one occasion travelled to Europe with Queen Zein.

But her travels are her passion and she writes of the places she has visited with a sense of wonder and curiosity that is inspiring, The pleasure of buying a duty-free steam iron at a border post and leaping into a bed in a rather dirty hotel room from the patch of carpet to avoid the filthy floor, stand out as much as the glories of Luxor and the disappointment of the reconstructed Babylon.

Her love of Jordan, despite all the modern changes and overcrowding shines through. Accounts of her trips to photograph the rich variety of flowers and plants in all the varied habitat of the country are among the best in the book.

Archie Hinchcliffe
WIFE OF THE BRITISH AMBASSADOR IN JORDAN
FROM APRIL 1993 TO APRIL 1997

Ann O'Neill belongs to a group of people, now rapidly vanishing, whose accidents of birth and background, have given them a view of the world with its extraordinary variety of histories and traditions, which is at once compassionate, informed, and yet firmly rooted in an Englishness we can still recognise.

So when she decided to compose a book of her life, from its early beginnings in a pre-independent Indian subcontinent through her many travels and long experience of the Middle East, it would be clear we would have a remarkable book to enjoy – fresh, observant, warm-hearted, and passionate.

For this is not just a personal history; it is (if one is prepared to engage with its panoramas of peoples and places) a plea for a way of living in the world of which we may all too soon lose sight – a respect for diversity, a dedication to the fragile wonders of the natural world, and a conviction that each human life, wherever formed, has a value that must be treasured.

Reverend Malcolm White
ANGLICAN PRIEST AT THE CHURCH OF THE REDEEMER IN AMMAN
WITH RESPONSIBILITY FOR THE NON-ARAB COMMUNITY IN JORDAN
2001–2007

We first met Ann O'Neill in the mid 1980s when posted for a three year assignment to the Middle East. Ann was well settled in Amman where we lived and became friends.

During our time in Jordan she introduced us to many delightful pastimes, trips to the Dead Sea to float in the buoyant salty water, and picnics in the desert or by the streams and waterfalls that tumbled into the great valley.

Ann was very knowledgeable about the wild flowers of the countryside which burst into life with the spring rain, and she captured their beauty in photographs and drawings which adorned the greetings cards she made and sold.

Her adventurous spirit was the result of her childhood days recorded in *The Gun Smoke Still Lingers*, a colourful account of her war-time schooling spread over many exotic locations. Her zest for life shows through in the exuberant description of Indian Army family life.

Later in life she revisited on holiday some scenes from childhood and noted with sadness how the political turmoil has greatly changed the locations which held such fond memories for her. *The Gun Smoke Still Lingers* is a touching memoir of a lost era.

Deric Bailey
SHELL AGROCHEMICALS MANAGER FOR THE
MIDDLE EAST IN THE 1980S

"Ann brings to us a wonderfully detailed view of life in India – pre and post-Independence – as a foreigner. This is a travelogue which stands apart from others in the fact that she lived in all the countries she has written about, and views them not as a tourist would. Her anecdotes, memories and personal experiences bring alive the cultural nuances and history of all the places she touches upon. Her writing has an old world charm, with its turn of phrase and a certain sense of intimacy with her subjects – both travel and people."

From Mrs Harinder Matai
A LONG TIME INDIAN FRIEND

Ann O'Neill and I travelled, driven by Ann's passion for the countryside, over probably every square inch of the Hashemite Kingdom of Jordan that was open to the public and quite a few that were not! (Military zones.) Her eye for detail, interest in history and enjoyment of the folk we met along the way made our trips memorable. On our drives and rambles Ann would regale me with reminiscences of her life in other parts of the world; she is a feisty and amusing story teller. Ann is a doughty old bird, not to be deterred by injunctions from the British Embassy in Amman that she stay in the capital city and keep a low profile when political feelings were running high. Off we would set through refugee camps and villages in the middle of nowhere, and, consequently, we had had the benefit of understanding of the political feelings of Jordanians and the Palestinian diaspora that was probably better than most.

I also travelled with Ann to India and I must say that reading *The Gun Smoke Still Lingers* brought the trip back very vividly. Her "photographic" eye re-conjured up for me the wonderful scenery and the characters we met. Ann paints pictures with words and her love of the countryside we were privileged to travel through resonates. The lovely thing about Ann is that she is equally at home in palaces and Bedouin tents and this informs her story-telling.

Ann is a committed Christian, but allied with a conviction that ecumenism lies at the heart of all her transactions with human beings, be they Muslim, Hindu, Buddhist or of other faith. I remember a time when we visited the city of Salt in Jordan looking for one of the many burial places of St George. He is venerated in at least twelve countries. Both of us were delighted to see an elderly Muslim woman, being helped down the stairs by her daughters – all well-wrapped up in their tradition gear – and a Greek Orthodox priest helping them on their way, after they had prayed for their mother's recovery in a Christian church. It is these insights that Ann has into the Middle East that make her book fascinating.

Diane Sellick – A FRIEND OF THE AUTHOR FOR FOR MANY YEARS,
WHO TAUGHT ENGLISH LITERATURE IN TURKEY,
OMAN JORDAN AND PALESTINE